M000003514

There are times in our lives when the things we may have dreamed about, hoped for, and even prayed for turn out to be the opposite of what we expected. Yet I am so glad that we don't have to live in mediocrity or survival mode just because life's circumstances may not be what we desired them to be. Yes, God has a plan, and that plan is to prosper you, not to harm you. His plan is full of hope (Jer. 29:11). As you read this book, Alvin shares from his heart, with humility, transparency, humor, and the truth of God's Word, how you can find the courage, grace, and the will of God—as He leads you on the pathway to reinvent your life.

—Darlene Zschech
Worship Pastor

In his book, *Reinvent Your Life*, Alvin Slaughter exposes his life and testimony in such a gripping way that many of us never realized coming from such a mighty man of God. He shares his story of reinventing himself to give courage and hope to others. He points out that our metamorphosis is only one step away when we come to the knowledge that it is only in Him that we live and move and have our being. Such frankness and candidness is very rare these days, but he has laid bare his soul to help someone who may be experiencing some of the same things he did in the early years. A great testimony of grace, power, and faithfulness of our Father God! It is NEVER too late to live your BEST!

—Judy Jacobs
Singer/Songwriter/Author/Preacher

Alvin Slaughter has blessed the world with his passion of singing. But in *Reinvent Your Life* he gently shares how passion must be shaped and combined with God-inspired planning to complete a worthy calling. Allow this book to help release your highest calling.

—DAN MILLER
AUTHOR AND LIFE COACH

REINVENT
YOUR LIFE

ALVIN
SLAUGHTER

Charisma
HOUSE
A STRANG COMPANY

1994, 1995, 1996, 2000, 2001, 2002. Used by permission of
NavPress Publishing Group.

Cover design by Amanda Potter
Design Director: Bill Johnson

Library of Congress Cataloging-in-Publication Data:
Slaughter, Alvin.
  Reinvent your life / by Alvin Slaughter. -- 1st ed.
      p. cm.
  ISBN 978-1-59979-608-6
  1. Success--Religious aspects--Christianity. I. Title.
  BV4598.3.S57 2010
  248.4--dc22

                                    2009051737

First Edition

10 11 12 13 14 — 9 8 7 6 5 4 3 2 1

Printed in the United States of America

This book is dedicated to my beautiful granddaughters, Lyric and Jazz, who are still young enough to think their "Papa" is brilliant and can fix any problem known to humankind. Babies, you light up my world.

CONTENTS

INTRODUCTION

I FINALLY REALIZED I HAD to stop pretending everything was OK. Because it wasn't. I had to quit acting like I had it all together. Because I didn't. That was the bad news. The good news was that I was learning it was OK to admit that I didn't have it all together.

The frustration and pressures of life that were coming at me at the same time from many different directions forced me to get real. They made me understand that it was OK not to have arrived yet, but it was extremely important for survival (not to mention success) to become *real* about the journey.

The reason I have written this book is that in my public ministry and private life I have met many people who are feeling the same way I once felt. When I experienced despair in life's journey, I felt paralyzed emotionally and spiritually to the point that, even though I sort of knew what I needed to do to make things better, I just didn't have the heart. I didn't have the faith, the fire in my soul to do anything about it.

That was when I was forced to get real in order to survive. It was that life crisis that brought me to a place of embracing the truth, taking responsibility for my actions, and, ultimately, experiencing the grace of God to *reinvent my life*.

There are many people writing books about personal development and empowerment. I wrote this book because empowerment, once my personal passion, has now become my burden for others. There are too many people who have retreated into an inactive, "safe" place for living their lives in a survival mode. Still, they hope life will change for them. They wait for God, for other people, or for a stroke of good fortune to give them the power to affect the change they think they need.

Sadly, they don't know that, as born-again believers, they already possess that God-given power for change, for personal empowerment, to walk in victory and fulfill their divine destiny. In my experience, they are not aware that they are continually giving away their personal empowerment while living a mediocre, defeated lifestyle.

If you think this scenario may describe your listless, humdrum life of discouragement or despair, I encourage you to face the truth. Jesus said, "And you will know the truth, and the truth will set you free" (John 8:32). Are you ready to confront your issues? Follow your heart? Find peace of mind? Believe the divine empowerment that is yours for the asking?

The truth is, your life doesn't have to be stuck in neutral because what you dreamed about, hoped for, and even prayed for didn't turn out the way you expected. You don't have to live in the mediocrity of survival mode just because life circumstances are not what you expected them to be. You can also find the grace of God for yourself as He reveals His power to you in *Reinvent Your Life.*

My prayer is that you may be inspired by a story that I share or a personal experience that I suffered as I struggled to face my issues. My goal is to be honest with you about my personal journey from failure to success in God, in relationships, in ministry, and in life. I have not arrived. My journey still presents incredible challenges. So, perhaps you can identify with my struggle and gain courage to embrace the truth that will set you free to live an overcoming life.

By the time I was thirty-four years old, I had seriously messed up my life. I had failed at most of my sixteen jobs, fathered two children out of wedlock, was evicted from two apartments, and suffered foreclosure on my mortgage. My financial problems led to two declared bankruptcies and an inevitable crisis in my marriage. I had lost a lot, and it didn't seem like there was any way to get it back.

When I began to face my issues and embrace God's truth, I am not kidding when I say my wife and I felt like we were reinventing life. In 2009, by God's great grace, we celebrated our thirty-first wedding anniversary. The years have brought seasons of joy as well as disappointment, but we can testify to the fact that "God causes everything to work together for the good of those who love God and are called according to his purpose for them" (Rom. 8:28). We have traveled the world together, living life-changing experiences as we have enjoyed getting acquainted with different cultures and observing life on the world stage. And we have grown together in our love for the Lord and for each other, as well as in the wisdom of God.

It was not always that way, as I have mentioned. Years ago, as I began to seek the wisdom of God, I discovered that wisdom can be defined simply as the ability to solve a problem. At times, I have felt like a reporter embedded with the soldiers on the battlefield of life. There, surrounded by common enemies, I have learned, through my own experience as well as through the experiences of others, to employ strategies that reflect the wisdom of God to confront every challenge victoriously. Make no mistake: I am aware that new challenges lay ahead in our future. But as we grow in wisdom as overcomers, we will not avoid failures; we will learn to confront them successfully.

Maybe your journey is filled with dead dreams, goals, failed relationships, and other debris of defeat strewn around you. You may have filled your library with books on self-help studies, steps, and principles, but you still feel powerless as you confront, or avoid, the challenges of life.

To help you reinvent your life, let me encourage you to receive the same supernatural intervention I received. Allow ministering angels to lift up your head to receive God's power as your own. The Scriptures teach clearly that if you have received Christ as your Savior, the same resurrection power of the Spirit that raised Jesus from the dead lives in you (Rom. 8:11). Wow! That is the essence of reinventing life!

What have you done with that power? Did you give it away? If so, it's time to get your power back! The greatest journey in life is to find the truth of God's love for you and divine strength of His power in you. Begin to ask yourself these questions: Who does He say I am? How does He say I should live? Why does He say I'm here? Inquiring hearts want to know. To seek God for these answers is to seek wisdom. And He has promised that all who ask for wisdom will receive it (James 1:5). What do you have to lose?

As you read this book, don't expect to coddle your pain or soothe your self-pity. Don't expect to remain in a defeated posture of impotence in your Christian life. I believe if you honestly pursue the truths I share that turned my life around, then your mind-set will be changed dramatically. You will discover your potential in God to overcome every obstacle to living a victorious, overcoming life.

Will you take the challenge? Will you confront the lies of the enemy and your own faulty thinking to tap into the divine power that resides within you and that will transform your defeat into glorious victory? Will you determine to stop giving your power away? To own your personal destiny?

If so, it's time to begin an exciting personal journey that will result in reinventing your life—starting now and continuing for eternity.

At the end of each chapter, you will find a section called "Making It Personal." I encourage you to prayerfully consider the questions there and open a dialogue between you and God and you and yourself. Dare to admit that things aren't OK, and I can promise you that you will begin your journey to *reinvent your life*.

CHAPTER 1

DISCOVERING YOUR
LIFE'S PASSION

H OW MANY PEOPLE LIVE their lives filled with discontent and frustration because they are not fulfilling their secret dreams, their God-given passion in life, their divine destiny? How about you? Have you dared to consider what you would choose as a vocation or set as a goal if you could do anything you wanted? What would it look like if you could *reinvent your life*?

I'm not talking about wishful thinking that bumper stickers proclaim, like "I'd rather be skiing" or "I'd rather be fishing." That is, unless you think you could become a successful professional in such a sport, establishing it as your God-given passion.

What I am asking is if you are working at a distasteful job for an hourly wage when you would rather be teaching students, treating the sick, or pursuing another secret passion in life. Are you living alone when you could be providing a home for a needy child, filling your home with love and laughter?

Is there something that you are passionate about but feel you cannot get involved in because, as someone said, "the tyranny of the present is enemy of the future"? So, you live in frustration, working to make the next paycheck, pay next month's bills, and try not to increase your credit debt too much.

I encourage you to think about the desires lurking in your heart and mind that seem too "impossible" to even articulate, too frightening to consider seriously. You might just discover the passion for life that is God breathed and that would bring you greater fulfillment in life than you ever dreamed.

There is hope for your happiness. As you choose to seek God's will for your life, you can expect Him to give you the desires of your heart, to discover your passion for life, which will let you enjoy His abundant life (John 10:10). Dare to take my challenge to dream again—I did; when it seemed hopeless, God gave me the courage to dream again—and then watch Him fulfill those dreams. With God's help, and a big dose of courage, you too can *reinvent your life.*

Discovering Passion Requires Courage

Recently I read a story about President James Polk, who came from a privileged family. He rose from being a lawyer to becoming the Speaker of the House of Representatives, and ultimately to serving as the eleventh president of the United States of America (1845–1849). Under Polk's administration, the United States expanded its territory by more than a million square miles with the annexation of Texas and the Oregon territories.

Yet, some have dubbed Polk as the "Slavemaster President," after a book by that title written by William Dusinberre. Part of the debate over adding new territories to the United States centered on whether slavery would be allowed or not. James Polk was a slave-owning politician. He had earned his fortune through the productivity of southern plantations worked by slaves who did not fare nearly as well as he did. Perhaps, to avoid blatant hypocrisy, he could not stand against slavery in the new territories.[1]

While his accomplishments generally rank James Polk among the better presidents, it is generally accepted that he left behind a country that was both larger and weaker— fatally torn over the key issue of slavery. Yet, on his deathbed, it seems his true convictions were expressed. After affirming his great love for his wife and leaving most of his estate to her, he asked her to free their slaves upon his death.[2]

What if Polk had summoned the courage to make that momentous decision during his presidency? How could his passion for the freedom of his own slaves have helped resolve the issue of slavery that almost destroyed our nation a few years later? We can only wonder.

> *There is hope for your happiness.*

The truth is, rich or poor, educated or illiterate, focused or clueless, when we reach the final day of our lives, we won't have to look far to discover our true passions; they will find us. Often, they find us later rather than earlier in life because we did not have the courage to pursue them.

Perhaps we feared the opinions of others or wondered if we would fail; perhaps we simply took the easy road rather than taking the challenge to become the person we were meant to become. Perhaps we failed to cultivate a relationship with God, who alone gives us courage and understanding to fulfill our passion, to walk in divine destiny.

God-given destiny is the path of ultimate fulfillment for every person living. There can be no satisfaction in life as great as knowing you were born for a specific purpose and that you are walking in your divine purpose, fulfilling the passion of your life. Yet, no one discovers his or her passion in life without experiencing the pain of overcoming personal fears, criticism of others, and many other "enemies" that try to frustrate our destiny.

MY PAINFUL JOURNEY TO COURAGE

As I read this conflictive story of a president whose belated courage could possibly have influenced our nation much differently, I considered my own life struggles. I remembered the love of performing music that burned in me from my childhood and my frustration that I could not pursue that God-given passion full-time, vocationally. I thought of my love for my wife, my son, and my daughters and the responsibility I had to

When we reach the final day of our lives, we won't have to look far to discover our true passions.

make a living for our family. Why were these life pursuits—music, ministry, and family—seemingly in direct opposition to each other?

I remembered the first time I received seventy-five dollars to sing at a church in the South Bronx. Was it a token of what could be? Could my dream of earning a living through my singing gift ever be realized? It seemed impossible. Then I thought about the devastating time when I had lost it all and never thought that I'd find my way again. My passions and dreams were crushed; it seemed hopeless that they ever would be fulfilled. Where would I even find the courage to dream again?

After graduating from high school, I didn't attend college. I planned to do so, but since I was already working as an assistant manager in the shoe department at the local mall, I figured I was one step away from the "big time"—shoe department manager. For a teenager, that seemed to be a gigantic goal for personal success and fulfillment.

From the time I was twelve years old, I was a thousand percent involved in my church and especially in participation in gospel music. Even after I married and began to have responsibilities of providing for my family, I tried to arrange my employment around my passion of participation in musical events.

At first, I worked six days a week in the shoe store, then at other positions in the mall. For years after that, I chose sales jobs, sometimes with commission-only remuneration because they allowed me to arrange my own schedule. My first priority was to be involved in gospel music; it was literally the consuming passion of my life. That was where I found my greatest satisfaction and fulfillment.

I have to confess that even though it meant neglecting the financial realities of my family, I made sure that I could be available for church musical events, rehearsals, and participation in various choirs and small groups. I loved singing solos for congregations. I loved to watch the people's faces as I ministered in music, singing songs about God's love and power. It was an emotional "high" for me to see grandmamas crying and young mamas dancing in the aisles. As God anointed my solos of praise to God, I was fulfilling my passion—using my God-given gift to bless others.

HITTING BOTTOM

There was one small problem. My family was suffering from financial lack due to my work ethic. I was a horrible salesman and made very little money through my sales jobs to provide for the needs of my growing family. I don't even have to tell you the strain this created in our home, especially as babies came and the needs of our family increased. I had not learned to walk in wisdom regarding my musical calling and my responsibility to my family, which was equally God-given.

My young-adult life was filled with mistakes that were costly to my future and to my family as well. By the time I was twenty-two years old, I had fathered two children out of wedlock. I married at age twenty-three, and a third child was born when I was twenty-five. By age thirty-four, I had been separated from my wife and children, had lived on welfare, had been evicted from two apartments, suffered a foreclosure on a house, was forced to go back home and live with my parents, had spent a night in jail, had quit sixteen different jobs, and had declared bankruptcy twice. During these years, I was still very active in church. It just seemed that my problems were bigger than my God.

So, though I had discovered my passion in music ministry, it was eventually crushed under the weight of life circumstances, for which I was largely to blame. Stress and depression, inevitable emotional responses to my bleak economic situation and strained relationships, were passion stealers. I didn't know what to do. My passion seemed to be at odds with the well-being of my family and was threatening our future. I did not pursue a professional music career because I lacked the confidence that I could do that. Truth is, I wasn't really sure what I could do.

If you consider closely my ongoing dilemmas in life, you will observe a pattern. The problem was not that God was not big enough or that He had forgotten me. Neither could I blame the devil or other people for everything wrong in my life. Though the devil and people are sometimes factors that need to be addressed, in this case it was my faulty life pattern that I had to ultimately face. That revolved around my own limiting mind-set, my poor choices, and my inexperience that hindered me from living the kind of life I desired and that would benefit my family.

Our minds are extremely important to our success or failure. The Bible teaches that we need to be transformed by the renewing of our mind and not be conformed to the mind-set of our culture (Rom. 12:1–2). My mind desperately needed to be transformed.

Even though I continued to pursue my passion for performing music locally, I did not find opportunity for it to become financially profitable as a vocation. My priorities needed to be changed. I needed to receive revelation from God of who I was and what His purpose was for my life in my family relationships and financial pursuits. That led to my experiencing a huge dose of unwanted "reality" that I have described.

Our financial situation was not the only thing to take a mortal hit by my failures. My faith was also shaken, my self-esteem hit bottom, and our family relationships were at risk. I didn't know whether I trusted God enough to answer my prayers anymore. It was a fact that I didn't trust my own decision making. Our future seemed bleak; it seemed that we had suffered one too many disappointments in our young married lives. Can you relate?

Reinventing your life requires seeking God to be led by

His Spirit and to receive God's blessings of divine knowledge, wisdom, and godly relationships to help us grow in our journey. In sharing my sometimes painful, humiliating journey, my only goal is to let you know that what follows is not mere theory or possibility thinking.

God's divine intervention and the lessons He taught me by His Spirit have resulted in reinventing my life, in living my passion, and in knowing exquisite fulfill-

Our minds are extremely important to our success or failure.

ment of my destiny. And it has done the same for my wife and family. My hope is that, as you follow my journey, you will receive courage and understanding to embrace these principles and that they will do the same for you.

A DIVINE VISITATION

I'll never forget the day I walked out of bankruptcy court for the second time. Just an hour earlier, I had sat motionlessly in the last row of that courtroom, wondering how in the world things could have turned out this badly. Relentless questions filled my tormented mind. "Where am I going to move with my family? What in the world am I going to do with my life? My credit is shot. My job prospects are slim. Furthermore, I'm not even sure I have the will to try again. Will I ever be able to pursue my passion for music ministry?" As I sat there, I prayed, "Dear God, I'm not sure things can get much worse."

And in that moment, they did.

While I was waiting for my case to be called, my head was down and my eyes were glued to the mundane view of my shoes. I happened to glance up for a moment and noticed a man staring at me.

"Hey, aren't you Alvin Slaughter?" he exclaimed loudly. "I love your music!"

I cringed visibly, desperate to escape such recognition. Oh, no! Now everyone knew I was "somebody." I felt publicly humiliated as my anonymous "cover" was blown. I responded weakly, "Yes, I am," and felt my last ounce of self-esteem hit the floor. With a patronizing look, my admirer replied, "Well, I guess it happens to the best of us."

Mercifully, my case was finally called. After some legal rambling by the judge, I was once again declared legally bankrupt. Some might conclude that it was not the worst thing in the world, but in my world, it seemed to be just that. As I turned to leave the courthouse, I felt like a big L for "Loser" had been stamped on my forehead.

To my astonishment, when I opened the door of that courtroom and walked into the corridor, the most unexpected feeling of euphoria washed over me. A wave of peace filled me, erasing my depression and defeat and quieting my tormented thoughts. I felt as if I had just received a prize. I looked around to see who was responsible for what was happening.

I had been prepared to spend the rest of that day wallowing in my self-pity, questioning whether prayer was really worth the effort, and doubting my ability to succeed in life. Instead, I felt comforted, encouraged, and free. In spite of the public humiliation of my personal financial failure, I believe God sent His ministering angels to lift up my head and fill me with hope. Only the love of God could have impacted my suffering psyche so dramatically.

In that moment, I remembered the words of Corrie ten

Boom, survivor of a World War II Holocaust prison camp in Germany: "There is no pit so deep that God's love is not deeper still."[3]

Though I don't understand how, in that moment of divine visitation in a courtroom corridor, God revived courage in me to take His message of love and empowerment to the world—through music. Somewhere deep in my soul, my future destiny was rekindled, though I had no idea how any of it would be made possible.

The Bible says that God gives beauty for ashes, the garment of praise for the spirit of heaviness (Isa. 61:3). I had just experienced that spiritual reality as God showed His love to me in His great faithfulness. Where I would go from here was to be determined by my response to His divine love and my willingness to "face the music."

Hope and a Future in Living My Passion

I knew that God had some kind of plan and purpose for my life. I really did. I just had no idea of how to find it and less of how to fulfill it. Secretly, I felt that God had left me to work all these problems out by myself, and perhaps I was not making it because somehow I just wasn't good enough or did not possess "mountain-moving" faith.

During the next weeks and months, the lessons I learned set me on a path to become a successful man of God, caring father, and husband who could provide for my family. They led me into open doors that enlarged my mind and made me an effective minister of the gospel through music. To the glory of God, I can only testify to His great faithfulness to teach, guide, and equip me with the wisdom and strength I needed to believe His promises and watch His power work to reinvent my life.

My only goal for this book is that you, dear reader, can relate to my pain, my progress, and my pathway to finding purpose and fulfilling passion in God's way. As you honestly evaluate your life, you can apply the spiritual lessons I learned. You can walk in the blessing of God on your life. The wisest man who ever lived said, "The blessing of the LORD makes a person rich, and he adds no sorrow with it" (Prov. 10:22). You can discover the blessing of God for your life and walk in His purposes, which will eliminate the grief and sorrow you cause for yourself and those you love when you walk in your own ways.

Reinventing your life will require taking personal responsibility. It will mean saying yes to the will of the Lord with all your heart, mind, and spirit. It will require that you refuse to continually walk in fear, worry, worldly instruction, and negative thinking. It means beginning a journey that will teach you how to walk in the Spirit, allowing your spiritual eyes and ears to become open to the will and ways of God. At first, it seems like a daunting task. But reading testimonies of others as you are doing—perhaps just one incident, one lesson learned, one example of transformation—can bring glorious transformation to your life.

By God's grace, what could have destroyed my faith, in the end, only made me stronger. The lessons I learned set me free from my fear of what people thought or what I had believed about my own identity. When the crisis had passed, my faith was stronger and my vision clearer. I could look in the mirror and know that I am a person of destiny, I am more than my job, and I am more than negative people's opinions of me or even my own self-defeating thoughts about my worth. I am a child of God, I am fearfully and wonderfully made, and

He has made me more than a conqueror in the face of life's challenges.

God continues to intervene in our lives with miracles when we need them. I believe, however, that perhaps the greatest miracle is simply a change in perception—of who God is, who you are, and what His provision is for your success in life.

KEEPING YOUR PASSION ALIVE

Once you discover your passion, you will spend the rest of your life nurturing it, watching it grow and change, and enjoying satisfaction of living your life filled with God-given purpose. Now, many years after my crisis encounter, my life passion, my love for God, my love for my family, and my pursuit of my divine destiny through my musical gift are all working together.

Reinventing your life will require taking personal responsibility.

Does that mean we have no more conflict in our lives? No more difficult decisions? No more questions? Hardly. But armed with a new revelation of who I am in God, I have determined that as long as I have breath, my passion will never again get lost in life's circumstances, in work, or in other related activities.

I put my trust in God, who gives me the courage to face down my enemies and fulfill my God-given passion. As I seek Him, He will continue to give me wisdom to meet the demands of family, church, and social commitments without sacrificing the well-being of those I love.

Not all life passions lead to a career or vocation, and you should not expect your passion to result necessarily in fame or wealth. But you can truly recognize your passion when you feel God's favor on your life and experience personal fulfillment in pursuing it. When you are living your passion, you sense a guiding focus, which is the hand of God. You disconnect from the mundane pressures of life and experience joy and contentment that make you sense your great worth. You can know that it is God given.

Every believer must make a determined choice to stay focused on maintaining his or her God-given passion and destiny. For many, that destiny is centered on raising your family. Unfortunately, many fathers and mothers who love their families and work hard to provide for them inadvertently allow their work or career to take priority over their family. They work harder to buy a bigger house or a better car. They work to escape the problems of life or to find the ego satisfaction their work gives them. When that happens, their passion for the well-being of their family becomes secondary to career, ego, or ministry.

Balance? I'm not exactly sure what that is. I do know that walking in humility before God and seeking His wisdom will keep bringing you back to the right priorities. Pursuing as your priority the God-given passions of your life will act as a compass to keep you on track in fulfilling His purposes for your life. I suggest that you seek to discover your passion for life earlier rather than later when you are ready to retire. Life is too short to waste on lesser pursuits instead of fulfilling your destiny.

I met a woman at an event in Rome, Georgia, some years ago. As I greeted her and we began to talk, I learned that she was a schoolteacher by vocation. But her true passion was traveling the world, teaching and caring for needy children in developing nations. I looked at the vest she was wearing, covered with patches that represented the different coun-tries she had visited over the years. It was amazing to see the sparkle in her eyes as she identified the country and told of the service that she had given to that area. Her passion for teaching and aiding impoverished and orphaned children who had run out of options was evident. Later in life, she had successfully incorporated her passion into her vocation, and she didn't have to start her own organization. She joined with one that shared the same passion she had for needy children.

LIFE'S PASSIONS CAN CHANGE

One of the most valuable things I have learned over the years about fulfilling God-given passion is that passions can evolve and change. As a matter of fact, during the course of life, they often do. This is an important lesson to learn to avoid disappointment and confusion when the blessing of God does not continue on your previous pursuits. That is why we must continually seek to deepen our relationship with God so that we follow His guidance moment by moment. (See chapter 3.)

As we develop in our walk with God, He is able to birth new desires and goals for our lives or channel old ones into new directions, current venues, or more effective applica-tions. When that happens, our journey seems to turn a corner, and we must sometimes leave behind what brought fulfillment to our lives in the past to embrace the new, God-given purposes.

For example, the teacher who traveled for years to third-world countries to help needy children later adopted a young child from Africa whose face had been disfigured as a result of an accident. No more traveling the world. Now, her passion is caring for one child and raising funds for the plastic surgery this child needs to restore her face. In that same way, as you strive to maintain your God-given purpose, you must allow the hand of God to guide you into new possibilities as well. Let Him strengthen your courage to live for nothing less than the passion He gives you to fulfill every moment of your life.

Music is not my only passion. I love to ride motorcycles. It's not a terribly productive passion (for me), I admit. But I literally feel God's presence when I am riding a motorcycle. It helps me to relax and think clearly. Some people love to study fine art and visit art museums. Others love to cook exotic dishes, or even not-so-exotic ones. Don't think your passion must be an earthshaking, publicity-filled event or even a vocation.

Your God-given passion could be that you are a great listener; people seek you out to confide in you their dreams, hurts, and questions. They know you will never divulge their confidence or deride their fears. You may be a great server, finding incredible satisfaction in helping wherever you see a need. It does not really matter what your God-given passion is as long as you identify it. What is most important is that whatever your passion is, that is where you find your heart's desire fulfilled also. The satisfaction that you get from connecting with your passion brings you a greater sense of well-being, spiritually, emotionally, and even physically. And this fulfillment of divine purpose will affect the quality of your life and of those around you in positive ways.

Life is too short to waste on lesser pursuits instead of fulfilling your destiny.

ACTIVATE YOUR PASSION

As we conclude our discussion of the importance of discovering and maintaining your God-given passion, let me give you some steps you can take to activate your passion. By taking these steps, you will be able to avoid the tactics of the enemy, and it will be much easier to overcome and resist the evil one. It is your responsibility to keep your passion alive, and doing these things will set you up for success and help you to head off any threat from the enemy to steal the passion God has placed inside you.

Avoid joy robbers

One way you can activate your passion is by understanding that the enemy of your soul knows how to undermine your God-given passion by specifically targeting it. For example, if you are a good listener, trusted confidant, and friend to many, the enemy will rob you of your fulfillment of that passion by sending someone to "dump garbage" on you. You know the kind. They just want to unload their complaints and unhappiness on someone who will listen. They don't want helpful advice for changing anything. They just want to vent their self-pity and gripe about life.

When you are bombarded by negative people, you need to recognize the enemy's attempt to wear you out and make you run from your passion for being a good listener. Learn to cut short those conversations, kindly, and use caller ID to screen future calls. You are not helping those people by becoming their "garbage can," and they certainly are not helping you by discouraging you to function in your God-given passion.

If you are most satisfied when you are fulfilling your passion for serving others, the enemy can discourage you by allowing you to be taken advantage of by lazy people. When you find you are too busy to enjoy life or to maintain your personal quiet time, consider what is robbing your time. Are you saying no when you should? Sometimes that means you are concerned about others' opinions of you more than you are of serving those whom God sends your way.

In fulfilling your God-given destiny, it is imperative that you learn to follow the leading of the Holy Spirit. The fact that I am a gifted soloist doesn't mean I have to be available for every wedding, conference, or musical event where people want me to sing. I cannot fear what they will think of me when I say, "No, thank you. I won't be available for that event." I have to be grounded in my walk with God and know I am submitted to His guidance in every situation.

If people take offense and do not accept my decision graciously, I have to forgive them and continue my journey with those to whom God sends me. There is enough pressure in living life; why take on more worrying about what people think of you? Living to please God will set you free from trying to please people all the time. Let your joy rest in knowing that you are obeying Him instead of allowing people to steal it by their disapproval.

Reach out—open your eyes, your ears, and your heart

Some years ago, when I was first invited to sing in Africa, my eyes and ears were opened to the beautiful people of that great continent, and my heart was enlarged. As I experienced their culture and shared their love for God, I realized that God had filled my heart with a love and passion for these nations I had not known before.

Whenever you reach out to someone where there is a genuine need, it will always connect your spirit with God's Spirit. Life is filled with opportunities where just your simplest act of compassion can change someone else's world in a big way. You don't have to wait for the big, the dramatic, or the organized outreach to fulfill passion and destiny.

Giving a smile, doing a kind act, and lending a helping hand can enlarge your heart with the love of God as you reach out

> *In fulfilling your God-given destiny, it is imperative that you learn to follow the leading of the Holy Spirit.*

to serve "the least of these my brethren" (Matt. 25:40, KJV), not realizing you are actually serving Jesus Himself. Do you want joy? You can reach out to help others and experience joy that you can't know any other way. The psalmist understood that reality when he wrote:

> Oh, the joys of those who are kind to the poor. The LORD rescues them in times of trouble. The LORD protects them and keeps them alive. He gives them prosperity and rescues them from their enemies. The LORD nurses them when they are sick and eases their pain and discomfort.
>
> —PSALM 41:1–3

Reaching out to others who are in need is a divine recipe for success. It takes your eyes off yourself as the center of your universe. It humbles pride and selfishness that keep you focused on your problems. Lucifer's fall was caused by his pride and selfish ambition to become greater than God. You can be delivered from that destructive trait as you determine to reach out to make others great, and you will be filled with divine joy as you do.

Learn to problem-solve

If I had sought God in faith for answers to my family's financial needs and to fulfill my passion for music, perhaps we could have avoided some of the painful years we suffered as a family. Instead of accepting our circumstances without hope of resolving them, I needed to learn the skill of problem solving.

I have learned that running away from problems usually just makes them worse. Avoiding problems compounds them, resulting in time wasted by stressing instead of problem solving. When we determine to face the situation prayerfully with a mind-set for finding a solution, God can intervene and give us a solution we did not expect.

It is human nature to seek the path of least resistance, which sometimes means putting off any problem-solving effort until the last possible moment. But you know you're going to have to face the problem eventually. So, if you take a deep breath, call on God, and face the giant now, you can free up your mind for other productive pursuits.

Even in practical tasks, I have learned to tackle hard projects at the start of the day. That keeps me from spending the rest of the day avoiding them and dealing with the nagging thoughts that I will have to get to it eventually.

Procrastination can rob your joy for all the wonderful opportunities life holds. I have found that procrastinators live with a false sense of "busyness." They are too busy to do the thing they are hiding from, solve the problem they are avoiding, or face the relational situation that needs to be resolved.

If you think that might be you, consider how much you are actually accomplishing in your busyness. If you're constantly busy with little to show for it, you are only fooling yourself!

A good way to make yourself accountable for your busyness is to write down your objectives. Then prioritize them and place them into a timetable. This practical approach to overcoming procrastinating will help develop the habit of getting a lot done and not feeling constantly overwhelmed. It's a great feeling to cross off the list of accomplishments one by one.

Problem solving is a life skill that is learned over time and with the guidance of the Holy Spirit. Refusing to develop this ability will inevitably result in a loss of joy and fulfillment in pursuing your passion. And it will negatively impact your relationships and your personal success. I encourage you to ask God to show you how to face problems in a timely way and apply His wisdom and grace to resolve them.

Be real about your wounds

My wife and I have a dear friend who, unknown to us, silently endured great physical and emotional abuse over the years. When she eventually shared what she had been through, she did so without tears. It was as though she was numb from her years of silent suffering, resigned to live a life of personal torment. Needless to say, she had lost her passion for life; there had been too many broken promises, painful blows, and unfulfilled dreams. She could see no way out. Why even care anymore? It hurt too much to care. The less it mattered, perhaps, the less she would suffer.

No one wants to feel pain. Chest pains might indicate a heart attack. A toothache may lead to a root canal or an extraction. But living in denial of pain, physical or psychological, can threaten life itself. Pain is an indication that something is wrong. On whatever level, it should cause you to make a decision. You should acknowledge that you don't want to feel that way any longer, and you must seek help.

You will never change what you don't first of all admit. Don't be afraid to say "I hurt" or "That hurt me." And when you hurt, don't be afraid to cry for help—to God, your pastor, a godly mentor, a trusted friend, or even to proper civil authorities. And cry as loud and as often as you need to until you find healing, restoration, and hope for your future.

I believe everyone should be vitally connected to a Christ-centered, Bible-believing, loving, and worshiping church. As a living member of the body of Christ, it is in this godly environment that we can find the healing we need. Besides your personal devotional life of reading the Word and prayer, you need to have the support of Christian brothers and sisters and godly leadership to help you face the challenges of life and overcome the enemy's attacks.

God's provision for believers' safety and spiritual growth is His local church. Just make sure it is not a legalistic, judgmental group of people who call themselves a "church." The character of Christ can be recognized in loving, forgiving, and supportive churches where truth prevails.

Let peace rule as an "umpire" in your life (Col. 3:15, AMP)

> *God's provision for believers' safety and spiritual growth is His local church.*

Jesus promised that we would live in peace in a troubled world (John 16:33). And not just any peace—He promised to give us *His* peace. He is the Prince of Peace (Isa. 9:6). What a promise! Why do so many people lose their joy and their peace in the midst of life situations? We have discussed some of the reasons, but there are perhaps as many other reasons as there are people.

We have to learn to let peace rule in our hearts. According to the apostle Paul, the peace of Christ should become the umpire that settles every issue (Col. 3:15, AMP). I have never seen anyone argue with an umpire—and win! He settles disputes with finality, and he is always right!

When you do not have peace over a decision or a choice, reconsider your decision. You are not in agreement with the umpire of your soul. Pray and talk with a godly counselor. Don't live life without the peace God promised to give to you.

When people rob your peace, consider your relationship to them. If friends are always creating chaos, don't let them rob your peace; not all friendships are of God. You have to get away from some toxic people. If what you watch or listen to is robbing you of peace, don't do it anymore. Let the peace of God rule in your heart.

I am sure there are many other pitfalls for passion that we have not discussed. But if you feel your life's passion lagging, getting swallowed up by life, or becoming less effective than it has been, begin to evaluate these pitfalls. It is not worthwhile to live life without fulfilling your God-given passion. So, seek God until you have direction once again, and then determine to walk in His way to fulfill your destiny.

Pray as you go

Cultivating a strong, consistent devotional life is a key to fulfilling your God-given passion and walking in His peace and joy in the Holy Ghost. When we pray, we can recognize the reality of God's presence in our lives. Prayer empowers us to be still and know God—finding guidance for every circumstance. Prayer is also our channel for submitting our lives, our wills, and our desires to the Father in reverence and humility.

Prayer is the pipeline through which we receive the joy of the Lord, which is our strength (Neh. 8:10). Without prayer, we cannot receive the wisdom we need to resolve the issues of life, big or small. We cannot hope to discover our passion or fulfill our destiny without a life of prayer. The Bible teaches plainly that we are to pray, in faith, and ask God for wisdom:

When you do not have peace over a decision or a choice, reconsider your decision.

> If you need wisdom—if you want to know what God wants you to do—ask him, and he will gladly tell you. He will not resent your asking. But when you ask him, be sure that you really expect him to answer, for a doubtful mind is as unsettled as a wave of the sea that is driven and tossed by the wind. People like that should not expect to receive anything from the Lord. They can't make up their minds. They waver back and forth in everything they do.
>
> —JAMES 1:5–8

Learning to pray in faith and receive God's divine answers is key to your success in fulfilling your passion in life. However, it is not the complete answer to your life problems. Like a two-sided coin, prayer serves a vital role in our fulfillment of destiny. The other side of the coin is just as necessary, however. That is *action*.

God always gives us choices, decisions, and responsibilities that are a necessary part of the equation for success in

God. That is why James went on with his discourse to say, "When will you ever learn that faith that does not result in good deeds is useless?" (James 2:20).

After you pray, you have to go. Begin to recognize open doors of opportunity. Make some careful decisions, prayerfully, and dare to believe God is guiding. Take steps in faith. They don't have to be huge steps. I'm not saying you should throw caution to the wind. What I am saying is to continue to seek the Lord, but as you pray, go.

Put away the fear of failure, of what people might think, or any other fear, and trust God to guide you. Fear just laughs at you when you pray and don't act. Too many people say they are just waiting on God when in fact God is waiting on them. He will open the way and show you the path of life—as you walk.

That is why David said, "Let me hear of your unfailing love to me in the morning, for I am trusting you. Show me where to walk, for I have come to you in prayer" (Ps. 143:8). He knew that it was up to him to walk after he prayed. Spooky spirituality that does

After you pray, you have to go.

nothing but pray accomplishes little of lasting value. God's purpose will be demonstrated when it is fulfilled in transformed lives in the earth.

Choosing to walk in God's divine destiny will require that you make the hard decision to "face the music." You will have to be willing to make necessary changes in your life in order to experience the satisfaction of living your life passion. I can tell you that it is worth whatever pain you suffer to make those choices. And God will be with you all the way.

Through your faith in God, you can break the power of self-defeating myths, the influence of negative people, and your own negative attitudes to live the fulfillment of your dreams. In a very real sense, you can experience the grace of God for reinventing your life.

MAKING IT PERSONAL

What passions for life have you lacked the courage to pursue?

What steps do you need to take to begin to pursue your God-given passions?

If you are still having trouble identifying your passion, answer this question: "What would I love to do even if I were not being paid?"

You can also identify your passion by considering the things you do now that give you a sense of God's favor. List them.

Reaching out to others is a powerful way to get "unstuck" in life. List opportunities you have to impact a child, encourage an adult, or otherwise give meaningful help to someone.

Describe your personality traits that form your identity apart from your career, job title, or other activities.

CHAPTER 2

FACING THE MUSIC

I T IS STILL NOT easy for me to confess my personal struggle with fear. For over twenty years I prayed and asked God to deliver me from fear. Fears of failure, rejection, my own weakness, and not knowing how to confront life's challenges plagued me continually. They affected every area of my life and kept me from success in life.

I thought that if God would somehow wave a wand and wipe away fear from my mind and heart I could live my dreams. I could become an inspiring author, a persuasive businessman, an award-winning songwriter, a successful entrepreneur, and a dynamic speaker—perhaps even a respected humanitarian or a fearless leader.

Though these lofty goals were admittedly out of my reach, I would have settled for Him helping me to simply feel comfortable in my own skin, secure in my own ideas, and confident in my decisions. If only I could stop retreating into the failure I was in the past. If I could just be free from fear to press into the future to become a successful person, I thought I could be happy. "Why wouldn't God do that for me?" I wondered.

Because of my anxieties and fears, I found myself continually rehearsing the dreaded consequences of my "probable failures" instead of my "potential successes" in all of life's endeavors. Trapped in this fearful mind-set, I was doomed to failure every day from the moment I got out of bed. It was a horrible way to live. I was a dreamer with great visions for life but no strategy, wishful thinking but no plan.

Eventually, after living my expectations of failure, even the dreams died. That's when I discovered that when dreams die, in a sense, you cease to exist. The person you dreamed of becoming has not become a reality, and you can't relate to the person you are.

It seemed like God had not come through for me. No matter how hard I prayed, how much I blamed God, how frustrated I became, how many times I threatened to throw in the towel, the dreams I treasured were not being realized in my life. Then I began to understand, little by little, that it wasn't God's fault I wasn't living my dreams. He was trying to teach me how to become an overcomer so that I could walk in His divine destiny.

Something was missing in my understanding of how to succeed in life. A powerful force was blocking my potential for fulfilling divine destiny. I was living my life waiting for the big break, waiting for God to release me from my fears, waiting for opportunities and open doors to present themselves, waiting for a certain feeling to hit me that would let me know, "This is it! This is my big chance!" Needless to say, that "feeling" never happened. Those opportunities never presented themselves, and my frustration increased.

As a professional singer, the phrase "facing the music" intrigued me. What does it mean to have to face the music? I have learned that it means simply "to accept responsibility for what you have done." As long as I thought God was responsible to do what I needed to do, I felt like a victim of life, of circumstances, and, yes, even of God's unwillingness to answer my prayers.

It would be awhile before I was ready to face the music, to take responsibility for my fearful state, my wrong thinking, and my personal failures. It would take time and require new understanding for me to agree with God's powerful will and positive plan for my life. But my seeking God would eventually bring the desired results, and in His great faithfulness, God would help me to become an overcomer and fulfill the dreams of my life.

> *When dreams die, in a sense, you cease to exist.*

RECEIVING POWER TO OVERCOME

Can you relate to my frustration with life? Are you living in survival mode, waiting for someone or something to empower you to become the successful person you want to become? Are you willing to change that mind-set and begin to take responsibility for your lack of success? If so, you will be able to receive the power of God to become an overcomer and be wildly successful in life.

What does it mean for a Christian to be an overcomer? It means simply to defeat the power of the enemy of your life that keeps you from fulfilling your divine destiny. Jesus promised that those who remain faithful to Him and overcome the evil one will reign with Christ forever and receive many rewards (Rev. 2:7; 3:12, 21). You have only two options: to overcome or be overcome. You must choose to become an overcomer in Christ.

As I have traveled in ministry observing the lives of Christians, I am convinced that many suffer this same defeating mind-set that I have suffered. In fact, if you were to offer me 20 million shares of prime blue-chip stock or one dollar for every believer who failed to reach their God-given potential because they were waiting for the right circumstances or the right feeling to hit them, I would take the one-dollar deal. Too many Christians live in frustration and defeat

You have only two options: to overcome or be overcome.

because of a wrong mind-set, a faulty expectation for succeeding in life.

The apostle Paul declared plainly that the resurrection power of the Spirit of God that raised Christ from the dead lives in all believers (Rom. 8:11). Yet, how many Christians live, as I did, under the captivity of some kind of fearful mentality that keeps them from appropriating the power of God? What is the answer to their dilemma?

We should need no greater divine influence to accomplish our destiny than to have God's resurrection power living within us. So, what is missing? What keeps us from becoming overcomers, victorious over every fear and negative force that try to destroy our future?

I learned that my faulty thinking was the most powerful negative force that kept me living in a cycle of failure—faulty thinking about myself, about relationships, about life, and even about God. Until we are willing to face the music of our own lack of understanding and wrong opinions, attitudes, and actions, we will live in fear and walk in failure. We cannot overcome the enemy without taking responsibility to release the power of God within us into every area of our lives.

WILL YOU FACE *YOUR* MUSIC?

As I was to learn, facing myself and owning my fears would be necessary for me to be free from them. Until I faced my music, I was giving away the power God gave me to live an overcoming life. Without taking responsibility for my faulty thinking, there would be no hope of embracing God's truth that would set me free. In denying His truth, I was denying the power of God resident within me. In a sense, I was giving that power away in preference for my own wrong mind-set.

Have you given away God's divine power in your life? How are you negating His divine purposes for you? What fears do you need to face in order to overcome them and live your dreams? Your fears may be different from mine, but they are just as destructive.

Perhaps you are afraid to get out of an abusive relationship. Maybe you live in fear of losing your job, displeasing your pastor, or disappointing your parents or your spouse. Instead of facing your fears, you choose to blame your boss, your church parents, your spouse, or other people for your lack of success, for your personal frustration in life, and for your broken dreams.

There may be some justification for the way you *feel*. People and situations can seem to influence your ability or lack of it to fulfill your goals and live your dreams. They can appear to be roadblocks to your success. But if you allow them to control your opinions, decisions, and expectations for your life, you are giving your power away. Instead of embracing God's truth and allowing the power of God to reign in your life, your fear of people and situations allows their assumed power to overrule.

In short, when you choose to embrace others' perceived

truths about you, instead of embracing God's truth for your life, you lie to yourself. In your fear, you deceive yourself and adopt a self-defeating mind-set. The Bible says, "Keep me from lying to myself; give me the privilege of knowing your law" (Ps. 119:29).

For as many believers who have allowed themselves to become stuck in these deceptive lifestyles, many others have found the secret of allowing the power of God within them to make them overcomers.

In this same way, you can overcome every obstacle to fulfilling your God-given destiny in life, and you can have the biblical testimony of overcoming the enemy of your soul: "They overcame him by the blood of the Lamb and by the word of their testimony" (Rev. 12:11, NIV).

Have you given away God's divine power in your life?

In facing *your* music, you will have to face some common myths that keep many people from fulfilling their life passion. But with the grace of God working through your faith, you will be able to overcome any lie the enemy throws at you. After all, it is the truth that sets you free.

MAKING IT PERSONAL

List your worst fear in life.

What does it mean for a Christian to be an overcomer?

Are you frustrated with life? List the main source (or sources) of your frustration.

Identify faulty thinking that may contribute to your frustration.

Are you willing to face the music? If so, what will that look like for you personally?

CHAPTER 3

CONFRONTING FAILURE MYTHS

SOMEONE ONCE TOLD ME that if I were hiking in the woods and came face-to-face with a bear, I should fall to the ground, curl up in a fetal position, and play dead. (Please don't put your faith in this unscientific advice.) The idea is that because bears don't see well, if you take this submissive position, you won't seem threatening and the bear will just lumber away in the opposite direction. I cannot be sure that this tactic is not simply a myth, and I would not want to risk my life to find out.

Yet, how many times do we place our faith in a person's opinion of who we are without knowing if it is true or not? How often do we risk our happiness, success, even our lives without trying to find out the truth of God about who He says we are?

Failure is inevitable if we are living under the captivity of our own faulty thinking or the wrong opinions others have of us. See if any of the following myths have influenced your life. If they have, I challenge you to embrace God's truth and defeat the power of the lie that has affected your level of freedom and success. Consider how your life could be different if you applied the truth of God to your life and released His power into every area of your life.

MYTH: IF I TRULY HAVE FAITH, I WILL NEVER FEEL AFRAID

Truth: Yes, you will! Great men and women of faith have felt afraid at times. In fact, some fears are healthy fears that serve as protection for you. We teach children to have a healthy fear of fire, of playing in the street, of bee stings, and of other potentially harmful situations. But besides numerous healthy fears, it is evident from the Scriptures that fear is not absent from the lives of godly people. The psalmist declared, "But when I am afraid, I put my trust in you" (Ps. 56:3). It was a given. David said he faced times he was fearful, and in those times, he chose to put his faith and trust in God.

It is how you react to fear that is important. The apostle Paul asked for the church to pray that he would have boldness when preaching the gospel (Eph. 6:19–20). Why did he need those prayers? Because he faced fearful situations. Paul endured rejection, physical beating, imprisonment, and even death in pursuing his passion to preach the gospel to the nations. He needed prayer to overcome his fear and to be bold in proclaiming the message of Christ.

When I read that, I had a lightbulb moment. I understood that fear is not just a plague of the timid. Even great men and women of faith and power are sometimes afraid. If someone like the apostle Paul, who had such divine revelation that he wrote much of the New Testament and established many churches, had to face fear, there is no shame that I (and you) have to admit to having fears too.

Greatness is not simply determined by accomplishing an incredible goal in life. It is also a result of your determination to face fear and conquer it with faith. Success in life will require that you wade through the raging waters of fear and come to the other side unharmed. God's answer to fear is to give you boldness to face it and to embrace the truth that conquers it.

I hate it when super-religious people make you feel like a second-class Christian because you fear something that they don't. While I agree with the saying "We have nothing to fear but fear itself," that doesn't make me feel any better when I am afraid! Only the truth of God's promises can set me free from the dreaded power of fear. And that can only happen when I discover and embrace the truth.

One wise, biblical way to conquer fear is to seek the counsel of godly people. Your pastor, mentor, spouse, or other godly person who has your interests at heart will help you think about major decisions and other life issues. The more secure you feel in making good decisions, the less afraid you'll feel. Seek wise counsel from people who have experience and a compassionate understanding in the area of your fear.

> *It is how you react to fear that is important.*

Many people who confide their fears in me have sought advice from unqualified friends, family, or anyone who is confident, opinionated, and can "talk a good line." You need to develop quality relationships in your life so that you can receive wise counsel (different from opinion) when you need it.

And when you do receive sound advice, do it. Prayerfully consider what you hear, even if you don't immediately agree with it. A lot of people only hear what they want to hear. That is not honest. Seeking advice is not the same as getting people to agree with what you want to do. Don't fall into this trap, because if you do, you're just lying to yourself, and you will eventually have to face the music for any wrong decisions.

Finally, don't become a wishful thinker. Wishful thinkers spend their time hoping things will work out, not putting effort into discovering wisdom. They make irrational decisions when they shouldn't and don't take proper action in situations when they should. Faith isn't foolishness, nor is it a shot in the dark. The Bible says, "Getting wisdom is the most important thing you can do! And whatever else you do, get good judgment" (Prov. 4:7).

MYTH: I'M NOT WORTHY OF SUCCESS

Truth: God says you are! Again, it was David who exclaimed, "O LORD, you have examined my heart and know everything about me.... You both precede and follow me. You place your hand of blessing on my head" (Ps. 139:1, 5). Incredible! God's blessing was on David in spite of knowing everything about him. Divine blessing has to represent the greatest success a human being can know. Jesus said He came to Earth for this purpose: "...to give life in all its fullness" (John 10:10). Sounds like success to me!

Some of us grew up in churches where someone may have prayed, "O God, I'm not worthy of Your goodness." It sounds humble, but the problem is, it is a myth. The truth of God's Word teaches that Christ made us worthy. Maybe you thought humility was to put yourself down so that you didn't seem like you were too boastful. That does not bring glory to God. Giving your testimony of how He has delivered you from fear and empowered you to live a victorious life negates the myth of "I am not worthy."

Some people have endured physical or emotional abuse

by someone they trusted or cared about. Their sense of self-worth has been impacted by these very real and destructive experiences. Others may not have succeeded at anything they have tried in life. As a result, they have resigned to a life of mediocrity. Their sense of unworthiness keeps them from even trying to succeed.

If you relate to these or other negative experiences that have given you feelings of being unworthy, I challenge you to embrace the truth of God for your life. He knows you—every move you make, every word, every thought, and every failure (Ps. 139:1–6). Yet, He loved you so much that, while you were still in your sin, He gave His life for you. When you receive His sacrifice on Calvary and become a believer, He makes you worthy. Believe it, embrace the truth, and drive out every lie to the contrary.

When I consider the blessings, the fullness of life, Christ has given me, it takes my breath away. I have a supportive family and a career to die for. I live in the land of opportunity, and I possess a glorious faith that was given to me as a gift from God. Do I deserve these blessings? Did I somehow earn them? No.

I haven't always been the best husband, father, son, or brother. I'm not the best singer in the world, and I sometimes selfishly take for granted the simplest, yet most profound, blessings in life, such as the life-sustaining air I breathe or the vibrant beauty of the landscape that surrounds me, changing from one glorious display to another as the seasons change here in the Northeast. Yet, God's love lavishly pours out one blessing after another into my trusting heart. His great heart simply longs to give good things to His children.

Similarly, my children are heirs of all that my wife and I possess now or will possess in the future. Should we die before they do, they will inherit the proverbial "farm." They didn't earn it. It is not theirs by any merit of their own but simply because they are my children. They bear my name, whether through natural birth or adoption. That is their qualification to receive all the blessings I want to give them; that is what makes them worthy.

God loves you absolutely and unconditionally. He demonstrated that great love through sacrificing His only Son, Jesus, on the cross. His death and resurrection show how much you're worth to Him. Even Old Testament saints knew the great goodness of God's purposes for mankind. God said, "For I know the plans I have for you…plans for good and not for disaster, to give you a future and a hope" (Jer. 29:11).

Redemption is not an intellectual fact that we can understand. It is a gift of God that we receive through the faith He gives to us. The next time you feel unworthy, think about this wonderful truth:

> God saved you by his special favor when you believed. And you can't take credit for this; it is a gift from God. Salvation is not a reward for the good things we have done, so none of us can boast about it. For we are God's masterpiece. He has created us anew in Christ Jesus, so that we can do the good things he planned for us long ago.
>
> —EPHESIANS 2:8–10

What an incredible truth, which is taught throughout the Bible, that God Himself has actual plans for your life, a divine purpose for you being here. And after your life here is over, He plans to let you live with Him forever. What a future!

You and I did absolutely nothing to earn all of this. I'm just one out of billions of souls on this planet. But you know what? When I sing to Him, I believe He sees only me—an audience of one. All I ever did was accept His love and ask Christ to be my Savior, and I was born again by His Spirit. That's it. Amazing!

The long and short of it is that when you say, "I'm not worthy," you are telling God, perhaps inadvertently, that you're more informed than He is. You are saying that He wasted His time in creating you in His image, higher than the animals, and that Christ's death on the cross to redeem you was a waste of His shed blood.

Reject this myth. Embrace the truth that God has made you worthy of His blessing. Then you will be free to enjoy your future in God!

Myth: I Can't Handle Rejection

Truth: Yes, you can! God's grace gives you strength to face the disapproval and rejection of others. The apostle Paul was persecuted greatly, and he declared, "For I can do everything with the help of Christ who gives me the strength I need" (Phil. 4:13). He understood that rejection is a part of life and that God gives grace to face it without fear.

> *God loves you absolutely and unconditionally.*

Much of my fear stemmed from wanting everybody's approval. When I was a kid in grade school, I remember a bunch of us guys were in the school gym during gym class. As a chubby (do they still use that word?), bona fide dork, I dared to walk onto the basketball court, where the cool guys were hanging out. I thought this might give me a chance to connect with some of the jocks, and maybe by osmosis some of their "cool" would rub off on me. Ahhh, I could be a ladies man! Super fly, you know what I'm sayin'? Just trying to get over! I had a couple of things going against me, but I felt confident that they were gonna cut a brotha some slack. (Please excuse me and indulge my early seventies' vernacular.)

I already told you I was a chubby dork. I also had another reputation I wasn't so fond of at the time. Everyone knew that I was a choir-boy Pentecostal. That meant that life for my friends and me involved no cussing, no dancing, no hanging out with the wrong crowd, and a whole lot of going to church. The other kids called us "church kids incorporated." My, how I loathed that title! So, I decided it was time to break that mold and get my hoops on with the fellas.

I will never forget that day in the gym. Nine guys loomed under the basketball net, starting to choose up sides. First, two team captains were chosen. Then, the captains chose who would be on their team. They started choosing alternately:

"I'll take Freddy."

"I'll take Louie."

"OK, I'll take Bobby."

"So, I'll take Oscar."

"Then I'll take Big Mike."

While they were choosing, I was praying, "Please, God, let him pick me. If You love me, he'll pick me. I'll keep my room clean. I'll get straight As if he picks me." When all nine cool dudes were picked for a team, my name still was not called. My heart dropped like a plane crashing to earth from 35,000 feet. They headed off to the foul line to begin their game, one player short of what they needed.

Of course, I couldn't let anyone know how bad it hurt. So, I just laughed as I walked away and said, "Hey, guys. Catch you next game." But inside I knew there would never be a next game... and there never was.

I don't know if my fear of rejection and my insatiable desire for people's approval was born that day on the basketball court or if it was just solidified there. I do know that I spent the next twenty years battling low self-esteem and dedicating my efforts to pleasing people. That painful gym class experience was eventually reflected in many areas of my life, motivating my decisions and actions, molding my relationships with others.

I hated rejection back then, and I hate rejection now. But by the grace of God, I have resolved the issue of rejection in my life. Just because in some people's eyes I may not be the right size, have the right education, or be the right color or the right whatever, I absolutely will not be denied the blessings of God.

As I have developed a quality relationship with God, I have learned to value my own opinion and sense of worth. We all have stuff in our lives that needs fixing. Some stuff is more apparent than others, but it's all just stuff. While I welcome constructive criticism from a small circle of professionals, pastors, and loved ones who truly know and care about me, I don't worry about pleasing everybody to keep them from rejecting me.

Many of our issues, our stuff, reflect deeper problems that are not solved in a day. Redemption is an ongoing process for a lifetime. My strength and confidence come from God, and He's still not finished with me yet. He's still working on me. And, in spite of my issues, He's also still working through me. He has no perfect vessels to pour His love and mercy into. In His mercy, He anoints us and pours His love through us to others as He works for our redemption. The apostle Paul understood this process when he said:

> But this precious treasure—this light and power that now shine within us—is held in perishable containers, that is, in our weak bodies. So everyone can see that our glorious power is from God and is not our own.
> —2 CORINTHIANS 4:7

I'm finding that self-confidence is useless. It is limited to the extent of what I think of my achievements or myself. God confidence is everything because in Him there are no limits. You don't have to play head games about who you think you are or what others think about you. When you walk in God confidence, you rely on the full force of the promises of God, knowing that He cannot lie.

When you feel like you cannot face rejection, begin to declare the truth of God's promise: "No, in all these things we are more than conquerors through him who loved us" (Rom. 8:37, NIV). Rejection is a part of life. If they rejected Jesus, they will reject you at times. You have to choose to believe the truth over the myth…and you will conquer the fear of rejection.

MYTH: I'M NOT A STRONG PERSON

Truth: Just because you're imperfect doesn't mean you're powerless. Even as Christians, we are all imperfect in many ways, but we are becoming stronger as we make right choices to continue growing in our relationship with God. The Bible says that when we are born into the kingdom of God, we are to be like babies who desire the sincere milk of the Word so that we can grow up in our salvation (1 Pet. 2:2).

Babies are weak and fragile and must be cared for diligently. Yet, with time babies grow and become more self-sufficient. They start discovering their little fingers and toes. As they drink milk and progress to solid food, they develop first into little children, then into active youth, and they finally become healthy adults.

The first time a toddler falls and bumps his head, he cries for his mama. But after many such falls, he begins to just shake it off, pick himself up, and get going again. Walking turns into running, and before you know it, what's not nailed down will be tossed down!

> *God confidence is everything because in Him there are no limits.*

To develop normally to maturity as a Christian, you will need to learn how to get up from your "falls" and shake them off to get going again. The Bible teaches us to walk in repentance and to ask for His help in every situation. This learning process cannot be avoided. It is a part of becoming a strong person.

As you dedicate your life to Christ daily, you will reap the reward of walking in His strength and growing into maturity as a godly believer. Don't use the myth of "I'm not a strong person" to excuse your immature behavior. Determine to grow in Christ and become a strong person.

Myth: I Don't Know What to Do

Truth: God promises to lead you into all truth by His Spirit (John 16:13). When you get connected to the source of truth, which is the Holy Spirit, He will reveal to you all you need to know to live victoriously. The Spirit of God is here to reveal Jesus to you (v. 14), and the Bible teaches that Jesus has become our wisdom (1 Cor. 1:30).

Of course, if you expect to live independently from God, this myth of "I don't know what to do" will become a reality. You can really mess up your life if you don't seek to know God and His will for you. That is when fear creates a stronghold in our lives.

Don't live in a vacuum! Many times when faced with fear, we retreat into ourselves. We try to figure everything out and save ourselves. We are not capable of knowing which way to go without the light of God shining on our pathway. It is very possible that the answer to your dilemma may not be inside of you; it may come from an outside source. Let me explain.

Many years ago I owed the IRS a lot of money. A business failure along with my own ignorance brought me to the point of tremendous stress that caused me to suffer serious insomnia. I didn't think I'd ever be free from this mountain of debt with its insurmountable interest accruing daily. I did not know what to do.

One day as I drove to an appointment in the city, I was so distressed I could barely think straight. I started praying that God would somehow supernaturally erase my debt—a rich benefactor, a check in the mail, a computer mysteriously erasing my little problem. While God can use any avenue to work His miracles, when He has something to teach you, don't expect such an easy answer to your problem.

I absentmindedly reached over and turned on the radio, thinking that music might calm me. But I didn't seem to be in the mood for music, gospel or otherwise, that day, so I turned the radio off.

I began to pray again, differently this time: "Father, would

You help me? Give me a plan or an idea. I'm not asking You to just make it disappear, because some of the debt is justifiably owed to the government. But with the high rate of interest and penalties constantly building up, I'll be ninety years old before I can see the light of day."

Just then, in my spirit I heard, "Turn on the radio." Not an actual voice, but like you hear a melody playing in your head. I just turned the radio off, but I turned on the music station anyway. Then I began searching the stations until I landed on a radio program on which an author was being interviewed. As I listened, I realized his book was about how to deal with tax problems.

I almost ran off the road! I couldn't believe what I was hearing. This author was speaking like he was talking to me. As soon as I returned home later that day, I bought a money order (I didn't have a credit card) and put it in the mail to order his book. I used the principles I learned from that book to greatly reduce some of the unjustified debt accruing to my account, and I learned how to set up a payment plan that I could reasonably pay.

This supernatural answer was more amazing to me because I couldn't afford an attorney at the time. Other books I had read were filled with so much legal terminology that they were of no help to me. By listening to that quiet voice and turning the radio on, God was able to show me what to do.

In that experience and others in life, I have learned to listen for the still, small voice of God...and to obey Him. He has promised to show us the way, to give us wisdom when we ask, and to provide all that we need to enjoy His abundant life.

I don't know where the answer you desperately need will be found, but I do know from experience and from the truth of God's Word that there is always, always, always an answer. And He will always give it to you in time to resolve your most troubling situation and give you His peace. It is that assurance that prompted the apostle Paul's instructions:

> Don't worry about anything; instead, pray about everything. Tell God what you need, and thank him for all he has done. If you do this, you will experience God's peace, which is far more wonderful than the human mind can understand. His peace will guard your hearts and minds as you live in Christ Jesus.
> —Philippians 4:6–7

Myth: I'll Be Misunderstood

Truth: That is a fact; you will be misunderstood in life. The myth involved here is really that you believe you cannot face being misunderstood. It may also be that you don't believe you can be an overcomer if you are misunderstood.

I have learned to listen for the still, small voice of God…and to obey Him.

Here is the truth that will set you free: You weren't put on this earth to win popularity contests. That's for beauty pageant contestants or politicians. This is real life, and in real life, your first priority is you. That means that you are to be concerned with understanding yourself and God's will for your life. Period.

When you allow what others think of you to control your decisions, you are giving away your power to become the person God intended for you to become. It is important to realize that being misunderstood, while it's not comfortable, cannot impact you negatively unless you allow it to do so. Don't spend your time and energy worrying about being misunderstood, allowing other people to control you in that way.

To be an overcomer, you have to lift your head and place your confidence in what God is showing you to do. Obedience to God will not always make you popular. If that is your goal, then you will be controlled by what people think of you. But if your goal is to please God, whatever the cost, you will become great as a servant in the kingdom of God.

Valuing greatness

An important key to overcoming your fear of being misunderstood is to value your own greatness. Mother Teresa, who founded the Missionaries of Charity and served the dying poor in Calcutta, India, lived a selfless life. Her primary task was to love and care for those persons in whom no one else placed any worth. Therein lies her greatness. Was she misunderstood? Undoubtedly. But it did not deter her from her mission; it could not diminish her greatness as a godly person who brought comfort to many.

Nelson Mandela worked for peace and stood against racism. He spent twenty-seven years in prison for that worthy cause. His dedication to justice, requiring the sacrifice of his personal comfort, reflected his greatness. Mr. Mandela told an audience, "There is no passion to be found playing small—in settling for a life that is less than the one you are capable of living."[1] He overcame any personal fear of being misunderstood, even being martyred, to live the life he was capable of living. Embracing his own greatness, he was able to bring lasting change to his nation—and to the world.

Every person who has accomplished great goals in life has

had to "walk the plank" to face their fears. On the other side, they have lived a life of fulfillment of their dreams and goals. When you have this understanding, you sign your personal emancipation proclamation and embark on a journey to greatness.

Activating the power within

The kinds of unhealthy fear we are discussing did not come from God. The Bible says plainly, "God has not given us a spirit of fear and timidity, but of power, love, and self-discipline" (2 Tim. 1:7). However, that power that God gives you will lie dormant within you unless you place a demand on it. You have to know the power in God's promise and activate it to walk through your fears in courage and with boldness.

Your faith in God's Word activates the power of God within you. He doesn't just wipe out your fears as you sleep. You have to use your faith, declare the truth of God, and rely on Him to give you courage to be victorious in your fearful situation.

Remember that we are growing in our relationship with God as a baby grows into a child first, then a youth, and eventually an adult. It is a process. As you use the measure of faith God has given you, it will become stronger and accomplish greater things to help you reach your God-given goals.

Don't confuse faith with wishful thinking. Wishful thinking has no true basis or power to bring you to a triumphant end. It's like romancing a movie star you'll never meet. It remains in the world of fantasy. Now, the object of your faith may seem far-fetched, unreachable, with all odds against you. You might be in need of a miracle to bring it about, but if your faith is rooted in God, just stay connected with the

Source of your faith, and He will give you your miracle. Real faith is strong—not weak—because God is strong. His power can defeat every fear you may face.

> *Your faith in God's Word activates the power of God within you.*

Fear impacts your life by paralyzing you, keeping you from living out the truth of God for your life. Some people say that you shouldn't acknowledge that you have fears because admitting your fears gives the devil a place to work in your life. I don't believe the Word of God teaches that. What gives the devil a place in your life is when you allow your fears to stop you from moving forward to do what God has told you to do—when you stop living with focus and passion.

Do you see yourself in any of the following scenarios? (Please see chart.) If you do, it is time to close the door to your fear and begin to activate the power of God that dwells in your life. You can be free from fear if you will agree with God's Word.

RECOGNIZING FACES OF FEAR[2]

Fear of failure

You can't move ahead or make a sound decision because things probably won't work out. You see all failure as fatal. No rebounds; this is the end of the road.

Fear of rejection

You can't risk loving or putting your feelings on the line. You've been crushed before, and it's not going to happen again. You sabotage any remote chance of healthy relationships, or you may be needy and clingy and will do anything to be accepted.

Fear of leaving the status quo
You don't try any harder than you have to because you can't bear the thought of not achieving your desired goal. So you just stay where you are, making excuses and convincing yourself that where you are now is just fine.
Fear of success
According to experts, the fear of success is rooted in the fear of social consequences because of our success.

My fear of success

Let me share how the fear of success impacted my life. First, it caused me to avoid decisions that would have given the goals I am passionate about a greater impact in the lives of others. I did not pursue the expansion of my ministry in this nation and other nations, for example, because I understood that the more successful you become, the more visible you become.

That visibility meant that my words and actions would be scrutinized more closely and by more people. I didn't want my sometimes controversial opinions and ideas to be challenged or misunderstood. I wanted to be respected as a person who just goes with the flow, not as someone who shakes things up. Who wants a singer with an opinion? Just shut up and sing!

If I were more successful, I thought I'd spend too much time defending myself for speaking the truth. Perhaps the ministry would suffer and even our finances would be affected. I was not sure I could pay that price for speaking boldly the truth of God's Word. I really liked being liked by people, and I made every effort to protect my likeability factor. After all, if I started saying things that were controversial, what would happen? Today, because my view of who I am has changed, I am enjoying greater success than I ever expected. I am free to impact my world for God without fear of what others think. I speak the truth that He shows me and am delighted when others are set free.

Success is not a curse; it is an opportunity to do more with what you are given. With success come greater recognition, greater influence, greater financial gain, and more opportunities to make a difference in more lives. Being successful does come with a price, which involves a sacrifice of personal comforts, a lack of privacy, greater scrutiny of your life, and other temptations that must be prayerfully faced. But there is no path of life that does not exact its price, especially failure.

I challenge you to confront the myths that are defeating your dreams and let your faith take you somewhere you have never been before. Let me encourage you to pursue success of your dreams and goals with all your might and let your faith in God grow. Look for opportunities to release the power of God in your life and into the lives of others. And dare to be great! When you give yourself to fulfilling God's revealed purpose for your life, you can literally make a profound impact in someone's life today.

Of course, every step forward to living an overcoming life depends on deepening your relationship with God. Strengthening this divine relationship is the only way you can discover your destiny and be empowered to fulfill it. As you love and worship Him, you learn to live for the purposes of God for your life. He designed you with a specific plan and purpose for you to accomplish for His kingdom. Your deepest satisfaction will be realized when you overcome every obstacle to walk in His destiny for your life.

As you learn to deepen your relationship with God, you will discover keys to your success that you will not know otherwise. Don't be afraid to trust His guidance, His love, and His direction. Get to know Him, and your faith and trust level will rise as you learn to walk in His ways. That will require that you face your fears, acknowledge them, and allow your faith in God to make you an overcomer.

> *Success is not a curse; it is an opportunity to do more with what you are given.*

MAKING IT PERSONAL

List specific ways the following myths have hindered your progress toward fulfilling your passion:

Myth 1: If I truly have faith, I will never feel afraid.

Myth 2: I'm not worthy of success.

Myth 3: I can't handle rejection.

Myth 4: I'm not a strong person.

Myth 5: I don't know what to do.

Myth 6: I'll be misunderstood.

CHAPTER 4

DEEPENING YOUR
RELATIONSHIP WITH GOD

DIFFICULTIES, OBSTACLES, EVEN APPARENT tragedies in a Christian's life cannot keep us from knowing God and walking in His will for our lives. In fact, most heroes of the faith have faced and overcome tremendous challenges that threatened to destroy their lives and futures. Becoming an overcomer by definition requires that you conquer potentially destructive attitudes, actions, and circumstances beyond your control.

The life of a Christian is not exempt from tragedy. In spite of terrible circumstances that you may face, you can become an overcomer if you choose to deepen your relationship with God in every situation you face. Joni Eareckson Tada is a powerful example of this reality. As a teenager, Joni loved to ride horses, swim, and otherwise enjoy outdoor activities. One tragic summer in 1967, her life was traumatically changed forever. Swimming with friends, she dove into a lake and broke her neck, paralyzing her body from the neck down. In that unexpected moment, she began an exceedingly painful journey to redefine life as she had known it.

As a Christian, Joni began to fight the battle, first for her life, and then to reconcile the tragedy that was redefining life for her and mercilessly challenging her relationship with God. Through her books she has authored, she candidly shares her struggle, her questions, her pain—her failures as well as her victories—in conquering the challenges she has faced to be an overcomer, living her life as a quadriplegic in a wheelchair.

Her overcoming spirit and deepening relationship with God are clearly demonstrated by her life success, the fourteen books she has authored, musical albums she has recorded, and the organization she founded called Joni and Friends, through which she works as an advocate for disabled people. Many receive inspiration from her faith in God through her daily radio program, and she is internationally known as an inspirational speaker and mouth artist.

In her darkest moments, Joni has found that the power of God within her could cause her to overcome her mental, emotional, and physical pain. She learned how to give His power to others and found that when it was released in their lives, it would do the same for them. Through personal tragedy Joni walked into her destiny and has not only found fulfillment in her personal relationship with God but also has impacted thousands of lives she could not have reached otherwise.[1]

You might have suffered an unfortunate divorce, the death of a child, or a bad report from the doctor. There are so many unexplained tragedies that can shipwreck the faith of a sincere believer. Your only safe recourse is to run to God with your questions and your pain. In spite of your pain, you need to know that your Christian life is not meant to be lived in constant worry or defeat because of circumstances and irretrievable loss.

Joni tells this touching story of a father who lost his son in a brutal murder. "He once wrote me and said, 'Joni, I used to have a million questions for God and no answers. I still don't have all the answers, but you know what? I don't have any more questions. Knowing Him is enough.'" She concurred, "It is not about whether we really know the answers to the 'why'; what really matters is whether we know the 'who'—the One who has all the answers!"

In the midst of painful loss, as believers, we can walk in supernatural peace. This sounds like an oxymoron—devastating tragedy yielding the peace of God. Our world at times seems to be spinning out of control even as we choose to believe that a sovereign God is in control. In the natural, it makes no sense. But as we determine to strengthen our relationship with God, though our emotional responses to the problems of life can overwhelm us, we find ourselves anchored in the love of God.

When we are strong in the Lord and His mighty power, we are safely resting in the will of God, in spite of our confusion and lack of understanding of our painful circumstances. Christians don't live by happenstance or coincidence. Everything that happens in the life of a believer should ultimately draw us closer to Christ and bring glory to His name. The apostle Paul made this astounding affirmation of the love of God for His children:

> And I am convinced that nothing can ever separate us from his love. Death can't, and life can't. The angels can't, and the demons can't. Our fears for today, our worries about tomorrow, and even the powers of hell can't keep God's love away. Whether we are high above the sky or in the deepest ocean, nothing in all creation

will ever be able to separate us from the love of God
that is revealed in Christ Jesus our Lord.

—ROMANS 8:38–39

RELATIONSHIP IS PERSONAL

The Bible teaches clearly that Christians need to become a
part of a local church, submit their lives to godly leaders, and
walk in fellowship with other believers. We need to receive
Bible teaching from the gifted men and women God anoints
as pastors, teachers, and other spiritual leaders. (See Ephesians 4.)

Having said that, it
is vital that we do not
default in our *personal*
relationship with God by
placing all responsibility
for our well-being on our
Christian leaders. Much like a coach, who can train the
athlete to build a strong body and teach him skills in using
it, godly leaders can arm us with spiritual truths and ways
to apply them. But in the same way a coach cannot personally apply the calisthenics to make the athlete's muscles
swell, neither can a spiritual leader apply the truth to your
heart, your thoughts, and your actions to deepen your relationship with God.

> *Christians don't live by
> happenstance or coincidence.*

While we should have the utmost respect for our Christian leaders, we must know for ourselves what the Bible says
so that we will not be swayed by every teaching and doctrine
that come our way. We should never become more enamored
with the messenger than we are with the One the message is
supposed to be about.

I've met too many people who are constantly running from

one Christian conference to another, looking for a prophet to give them a "word from the Lord." They are searching for that magic touch that will beat up the devil and give them instant solutions to their problems.

Conferences can be great sources for information and inspiration for Christians. And the gift of prophecy can be a wonderful biblical encouragement when exercised wisely by mature spiritual leaders. However, these are not supposed to be a substitute for knowing God for yourself. According to the Scriptures, relationship with God is intimately personal.

If you are dependent on others for your spiritual "muscle," let me encourage you to retrieve the power you have given away to them. Get your personal relationship with God back on track. The Bible declares that those who seek Him will find Him (Prov. 8:17). Above all else, God wants you to know Him as your personal Savior, your Father, your Shepherd, your Provider, and your Lord.

GET YOUR DEVOTIONS BACK

Even if you attend a great church with mature, godly leadership, you must still personally take all the good they have deposited into you and apply it *personally.* That is God's plan for you so that you can serve God and experience the joy of your personal relationship with Him. Your relationship with God can be no stronger than your personal knowledge and application of the Word of God to your life. You must release your faith to see the power of God released in your life and situations.

God is not calling for us all to be theologians, delving into the original Hebrew and Greek languages in which the Bible was written. He doesn't expect you to understand the entire history of the Byzantine Empire, the Roman Empire, or any other culture. But when you hear a Bible message preached, don't just jot notes down and file them away. Take them to your private devotional time, read them again, and let the Holy Spirit guide you as you study the Word yourself.

GET YOUR PRAYER LIFE BACK

You cannot allow others to control and dictate whether you hear from God or not. "Am I praying enough? What should I do with my life? I'm not fulfilled." You will never become strong in faith by letting others control you or by seeking everybody's approval. Your pastor, your boss, your co-workers, and even your family members are not to become substitutes for your own brain.

Through personal prayer and waiting on God, you can expect the Holy Spirit to illuminate your mind and show you the pathway through the most difficult struggle you face. The Scriptures teach this fact clearly:

> Trust in the LORD with all our heart; do not depend on your own understanding. Seek his will in all you do, and he will direct your paths.
>
> —PROVERBS 3:5–6

Of course, God will use your relationship with others to speak into your life, but the ultimate responsibility of how you live your Christian life is personal. In that regard, you will never stand before God and use others as an excuse for your personal failure to know God or do His will.

When God asks you to pray, He's not calling you to a boring, tedious, repetitive, one-sided conversation. It shouldn't be as though you are talking to some stuffy, distant, uncaring dignitary who has better things to do than listen to your problems. When you are talking to the Father, you are addressing the one who made you in His image, the one who is called Love, and the one who cares deeply about your life.

God is not waiting for you to pray so that He can call you on the carpet for every little thing you did or did not do correctly. Unfortunately, because many people establish their concept of who God is from human relationships that are extremely flawed, it takes time to get to know this loving Father for who He really is. But that is precisely why He asks you to seek Him and find Him. He wants to surprise you with the delights that only a heavenly Father can bestow on your life. John, the beloved disciple, gives an extraordinary glimpse into the loving character of God:

> *Relationship with God is intimately personal.*

> What marvelous love the Father has extended to us! Just look at it—we're called children of God! That's who we really are. But that's also why the world doesn't recognize us or take us seriously, because it has no idea who he is or what he's up to.
>
> —1 JOHN 3:1, THE MESSAGE

When you fail to develop your relationship with God through regular private prayer, your spiritual muscles cannot develop. Worry and fear attack your mind and your emotional life, and you become paralyzed by negative thinking. In that mental state, it is difficult to pray.

Overcoming persistent worry

Persistent worry is detrimental to the believer because it replaces persistent prayer. Worry doesn't motivate God to move on your behalf. However, God will move heaven and Earth when you pray in faith according to His will (1 John 5:14–15).

The Bible says that pride keeps a person from seeking God (Ps. 10:4). It declares that God looks favorably on the humble to hear their cry and help them (Ps. 10:17). It is clear that if you choose not to pray and to rely only on your ego with its selfish, proud desires and purposes, you will not know God. You will not know His will for your life, and you will be headed for disaster.

So, then, how do we know His will? We know His will by humbling ourselves to seek God and yielding to His Holy Spirit. You have to get rid of your ego if you truly want to walk in the Spirit. How do you know you're walking in the Spirit and not your ego? I'm glad you asked.

If you are not choosing to live God's way through learning what His Word teaches and seeking Him in prayer, you are putting your confidence in your ego and what seems best for you according to your natural desires and feelings. You lay aside your ego in part by bowing before God and asking Him to show you the way He wants you to live in every situation.

The apostle Paul shows us how this works:

> What happens when we live God's way? He brings gifts into our lives, much the same way that fruit appears in an orchard—things like affection for others, exuberance about life, serenity. We develop a willingness to stick with things, a sense of compassion in the heart, and a conviction that a basic holiness permeates

things and people. We find ourselves involved in loyal commitments, not needing to force our way in life, able to marshal and direct our energies wisely. Legalism is helpless in bringing this about; it only gets in the way.
—GALATIANS 5:22–23, THE MESSAGE

The way to overcome defeat in the face of a painful divorce, teenagers acting like aliens from outer space, IRS audits, unexpected job loss, sickness, or accident is to never, ever let your life get so full that you don't find the time to seek God in prayer and meditation. Carve out space, and make a place in your life to meet daily with God. It may mean taking a walk at lunchtime. It may be driving to and from work. It could be sitting in your recliner in the privacy of your basement.

> *The ultimate responsibility of how you live your Christian life is personal.*

Choose a time and place to seek God, and you can expect Him to meet you there. The Bible refers to these private encounters as dwelling in the secret place. God's voice is amplified to our spirit as we linger there, quietly waiting in His presence. Intimate communion with God can only be found in the secret place. It is there that we can truly become still and know that He is God (Ps. 46:10). No matter the situation you are facing, His presence will empower you to know how to overcome and to become the conqueror He has ordained that you become.

Religious praying that says only what you feel is politically correct is useless. Remember, prayer is conversing with God, so forget about style, and focus on being transparent with your Father. You're not praying powerless prayers to an impotent God, but life-changing prayers to our all-powerful God (Isa. 37:15–16)!

As you humble yourself to wait on God consistently in prayer, He will open every door that should be opened for you to walk in destiny. And He will close those doors that should be closed so that you will not choose a wrong path.

Personal responsibility required

What we pray for is also very important. Don't ask God to help make life easier. Ask Him to help make you better. It is possible to ask for the wrong outcome, which leads to disappointment. One of the worst disappointments you can experience is when you pray for something specific and it does not turn out the way you expected.

But that does not mean that God did not hear your prayer. It simply means that He is responding to you based on His purposes that will ultimately turn out for much greater good. Praying does not just involve making requests like taking a shot in the dark. Prayer positions you in the will of the Father and moves Him to work on your behalf. The answer to prayer often requires personal action.

Before I went bankrupt years ago, most of my prayers consisted of asking God to meet my basic needs. I was just trying to survive, so I prayed, "Lord, help me pay my bills. Oh God, make my children do well. Help my marriage out. Lord, take away these problems." While it was positive that I was praying and asking God for help, He had to teach me some valuable lessons about prayer and about life.

You see, God doesn't write out checks to pay bills. We do! Neither does He train our children or make us treat our spouse right. The Bible provides the road map. The Holy

Spirit will be our guide, but we are the ones behind the wheel of the car. For example, we can't expect God to do what He has taught us in His Word that is our part to do. If we are creating problems in our marriage, He can show us where we are wrong, but He can't fix it if we don't change and repent for our failure. That is our part.

Now, miracles do happen. Many of us are walking miracles, and I see them all the time. But waiting for miracles is not an excuse for irresponsibility. You can't live your life chasing miracles without knowing what God expects from you. That is why you cannot expect to be an overcomer without deepening your relationship with God through studying His Word and developing a personal prayer life.

> *We know His will by humbling ourselves to seek God and yielding to His Holy Spirit.*

When I was in debt, I was looking for the "miracle man" with a miracle check to make me miraculously debt free. I was praying for my kids to miraculously get As in school. I was looking for God to miraculously make my wife realize that I am the king, the big kahuna, and what I say is law—no questions asked! No personal action required here!

I'm so glad I didn't hold my breath waiting for those miracles to come to pass. God did give us miracles. He did answer my prayers. But when answers came, they were a result of my deepening relationship with God. They involved prayer, personal action, focus, discipline, learning to make right decisions, and, above all, God's faithfulness.

The answers God gave were based on the abundance of His promises, not on my small mentality. He doesn't just promise to help you survive in this world. He wants to give you the desires of your heart (Ps. 37:4–5), and His chief goal is to make you the person He ordained for you to be.

For example, after I experienced ultimate financial failure and declared bankruptcy, I began to pray differently. Instead of just asking Him to meet my needs, I asked God to give me my heart's desire. I applied His Word to my situation, acknowledging that He promises to give me the desires of my heart. So, I prayed something like this:

> *Prayer positions you in the will of the Father and moves Him to work on your behalf.*

> *Lord, give me the wisdom I need to make wise decisions to work through my problems. Make me a man of God who can help to build Your kingdom around the world through my gift in music, in business, by my life testimony, and in whatever I put my efforts to do. I ask for abundance in my marriage and my finances so that we can give of ourselves and our abundance to others as You lead, even if that means making personal sacrifices so that others can be blessed. I pray that my children will excel in life and in their deep love of You. Help me to be a godly example to my family and to all those with whom I come into contact.*

Out of the depths of my personal pain, I began to pray fervently for God's divine provision, praying from the heart, which is where our true emotions live, and not from the head. Head prayers are prayers that you think will impress people and will show God how knowledgeable you are.

God is the master Creator; He owns it all. He is not limited by time and human boundaries. He's kind of hard to impress! But of all the things in the universe that the Father has created for His pleasure, the one thing He wants more than all of that is your heart.

He leaves that up to you. Only as you humble yourself, give your heart to God, and seek Him through prayer can God receive His heart's desire. God's desire is for an ever-deepening relationship with you, heart to heart. Don't be concerned about telling God what's really in your heart, even if it's not pretty. He knows it already, and He won't be put off. He can handle it when you give it to Him, and His Spirit will steer you in the right path.

A majority of the psalms that David wrote involve his gut-level, transparent cry for help. Yet, even with all his wrangling with God, his brutal honesty, the Scriptures say that God called him a man after God's own heart (Acts 13:22). David's honesty did not jeopardize his relationship with God; it proved that he was indeed after God's heart.

The Scriptures teach that you have the same power of God dwelling in you that raised Jesus from the dead (Eph. 1:18–20). To activate that power, you will need to accept that reality and begin to exercise the divine authority you have been given. You cannot wait for someone else to do that for you. Personal action is required.

It would be ridiculous to get up in the morning, dress yourself, start your car, and then get out and hop into the backseat, waiting for someone else to take the wheel and drive you to your destination (unless you have a chauffeur). But in a sense, that's the way many of us live our lives. We know we have a car, we get into it, we start the engine, but then we refuse to do our part to drive where we need to go. We know we are in Christ, that He has empowered us to live, but we don't activate that power through our thoughts, decisions, and actions.

For example, how many people are waiting for a miracle to increase their annual income when they are stuck in a dead-end, minimum-wage job? Instead, they need to seek God for direction, expect to get more training and education, and walk through open doors for apprenticeship or some other practical means of increasing their productivity.

> *God's desire is for an ever-deepening relationship with you, heart to heart.*

If you're in an abusive relationship, you don't have to wait for a sign from heaven to tell you to get out of harm's way. The full force of heaven will guide you, but you can't wait for the abuser to tell you when it's time to leave. And you can't decide to believe the promises you have heard before that everything will be different when you come back.

Personal action requires that you determine to take the lead in finding the path God has ordained for you. We should all aspire to lead. It doesn't matter if you never lead a Fortune 500 corporation or an international ministry, but you need to be able to push yourself to a better career or business. Lead yourself out of destructive and unhealthy relationships.

Lead yourself out of unproductive busyness and needless commitments that don't fulfill your destiny in God. Lead yourself out of being an enabler for others, serving them as their counselor or banker or shoulder to cry on. The false comfort you offer others may keep them from taking respon-sibility to seek God for a deeper relationship. You may very well be hindering somebody from getting his or her own power back, offering them yours instead. If this sounds familiar, it is time to release them to fulfill their destiny.

You may be thinking this sounds selfish not to try to help everyone who asks for help. After all, God said to love your neighbor as you love yourself (Matt. 22:39). But the truth is, unless you are led by the Spirit even in helping others, you will exhaust yourself and burden yourself with the weight of everyone's problems. Is that loving yourself? I don't think so.

It is important that you ask God to help you take charge of your life and let God do His job in the lives of other people. You cannot be their savior. As you learn to hear the voice of God, He will show you what is important in your life and what is not. Stop giving your power away to people who refuse to seek God for themselves.

Don't sacrifice your power to unhealthy habits and emotions. Stop seeing yourself as powerless when God sees you as more than a conqueror. God's power is not confined to the heavens. God's power is in you! He is waiting to show you how to activate it through prayer and deepening your relationship with Him.

GET YOUR JOY BACK

The greatest joy you can know is the joy God gives to those who pursue relationship with Him. That joy is the source of your strength in God (Neh. 8:10). There are too many joyless Christians filling churches today. We need to ask ourselves why we are not experiencing the promises of God for peace and joy in the Holy Ghost (Rom. 14:17).

Unresolved and unrepented sin can steal your joy (Ps. 51:8). What you constantly feed your mind can also steal your joy. I used to watch the news on TV first thing in the morning and then listen to the news and talk radio in my car while driving. At the end of the day, I'd watch the news again before going to bed. I'd filled my mind with news about war, terrorism, child abuse, murder, and all kinds of political wrangling. I would hear the same bad stories dissected and rehashed over and over again. No wonder I was filled with anxiety, biting my nails and eating lots of junk food!

There really is a lot of good that is going on in our world. There are people kicking drug addictions every day. Families are still being restored. Abuse victims are speaking out. Criminals are being prosecuted. Advances against cancer and other deadly diseases are being made in science and medicine.

I think the media are definitely lopsided. They say that good news won't get the ratings, but I would beg to differ. Someone should take the challenge and create a balance in favor of good news. But meanwhile, I refuse to let a steady diet of bad news steal my joy. I still listen to the news, but not all the time.

> *Unless you are led by the Spirit even in helping others, you will exhaust yourself and burden yourself with the weight of everyone's problems.*

I spend my days, whether in the office, at home, in my car, or on a plane, singing and listening to things that bring me pleasure. In my iPod, I have everything from Kirk Franklin to The Stylistics. I also listen to conferences with speakers who share faith-building messages—and not just preaching conferences but marketing, business, writing, and motivational conferences as well.

In my spare time, I love reading books and stories about people who survived horrendous situations. I also have photos of my family on my computer and cell phone that I glance at throughout the day. They fill my mind and heart with joy. In short, I surround myself with good food for my mind.

The absolute best thing to do to maintain the joy of the Lord is to get into His presence. The psalmist knew this secret when he wrote, "You will show me the way of life, granting me the joy of your presence and the pleasures of living with you forever" (Ps. 16:11). This reality of His presence is so much more than just the realization that God exists in the world.

I'm talking about opening a channel for the presence of God to become an integral part of your world—a place where you know that God knows you and hears you and feels you. When I come into His presence, I sing songs to Him and about Him. I'm learning to meditate and think on things that are pure, lovely, and admirable—things that are excellent and worthy of praise (Phil. 4:7–8).

Sometimes I have to remind myself to think this way. It's so easy to let the feelings of fear and a sense of being overwhelmed by life's challenges overrule your joy. I remind myself that God is on my side, and with Him, I have more empowerment than any enemy, even if the whole world is against me. (I hope I don't ever have to face that!)

GET YOUR WORSHIP BACK

I am concerned that too many Christians view worship through their experience of singing songs at church. Too much of our church worship has shrunk to "diet Jesus" or "fast-food" sermons with mediocre entertainment with a dash of refried preaching or a teaching series that my head already knows but still leaves my spirit empty.

I'm not referring to a particular style of worship or length of services necessarily. When you go to church or have a small-group meeting with believers, worship needs to be more than songs led by an enthusiastic worship leader and a three-point sermon timed to end appropriately. It needs to involve me personally, not as a spectator of TV or the Internet. Jesus said the greatest commandment was to love God with all your heart, mind, soul, and strength.

Don't get me wrong; I enjoy some of my best times of worship when I'm alone. I can receive inspiration from sermons on the Internet or gospel music on TV, and my life can be impacted. But nothing is a substitute for corporate worship with like-minded believers who are worshiping God in Spirit and in truth together. When we join our hearts and our voices together in unhindered praise to God, His presence dwells among us in a special way.

I love going to the theater. I love going to restaurants. I love hanging with loved ones. (I tolerate shopping.) Those are all activities we can enjoy in life, but being a part of God's kingdom is so much more than just the mundane thing we call life. It is a supernatural encounter with the Spirit of God. Praise and worship lead us into that encounter again and again. Fellowship with believers around worship is to be a consistent practice for every Christian who wants to cultivate the joy of the Lord.

A life filled with obedience and the joy of the Lord will be a strong witness to others who walk in darkness. The apostle Paul said to the Philippian church:

Dearest friends, you were always so careful to follow my instructions when I was with you. And now that I am away you must be even more careful to put into action God's saving work in your lives, obeying God with deep reverence and fear. For God is working in you, giving you the desire to obey him and the power to do what pleases him. In everything you do, stay away from complaining and arguing, so that no one can speak a word of blame against you. You are to live clean, innocent lives as children of God in a dark world full of crooked and perverse people. Let your lives shine brightly before them. Hold tightly to the word of life, so that when Christ returns, I will be proud that I did not lose the race and that my work was not useless.

—PHILIPPIANS 2:12–16

GET YOUR MIND BACK

You are probably aware, in our psychology-based society, that your mind is filled with thousands of images and experiences, good and bad, of what you have lived in the past. You didn't have loving parents, or you faced ridicule or abuse when you were a child. You suffered a tragic loss of a loved one or lived in anxious fear of not having enough. All that "data" is still stored somewhere in your mind.

If you grew up hearing harsh, legalistic preaching that emphasized outward appearance and lists of rules for salvation, your mind may still be clogged with negative attitudes and resentment. If you were made to feel that you were never good enough or "saved" enough, those self-esteem issues may have clogged the filter of your mind.

One of the reasons some people with weight issues find it so difficult to lose weight is that they suffer from an unhealthy self-image and low self-esteem. Emotional or stress eaters think that if they just lose the weight then they'll have greater self-esteem. That is simply not true.

In fact, for emotional eaters to lose weight effectively, they must become aware of their personal value and self-worth. Without that dynamic change in perspective, weight loss will be a yo-yo experience at best. Every time they face a situation that rattles their emotions, their typical response will be to eat comfort foods, gain back the weight they lost, and experience lower self-esteem as a result. The only long-term solution to weight loss is to get your mind back, to cultivate relationship with God, and to learn how valuable you are to Him. Then, with your self-esteem intact, you can face the challenge successfully to conquer weight loss.

Couples faced with marital problems sometimes consent to get counseling if they both want to save their marriage. Some attend marriage seminars, while others read books to help find answers and solutions to the problems we sometimes face when two hearts become one. I recommend a life-changing resource that you can find at www.hopeforthemarriage.net. It is a powerful resource that will help you develop stronger relationships.

However, I believe that you should work on your personal relationship with God even more than you work on your marriage. Ultimately, developing a deeper relationship with God will result in a stronger marriage. Find out what things in your past have clogged your mind and what baggage you have brought into your marriage. If you work on cleaning out all the self-defeating junk in your mind, you'll become a happier person.

You will find peace and joy in God and learn how He wants you to live. Walking in divine destiny, you will find personal fulfillment. You will be less defensive, more patient, more forgiving, and able to esteem others higher than yourself. You won't feel threatened by your relationships, feeling they're getting the upper hand.

Deepening your personal relationship with God is the key to healthy relationships. Why? Because no matter how much teaching you listen to and how much truth you hear, if it is filtered through a clogged mind that says, "That's not for me," then you will never get your power back. When you hear the truth—"We are more than conquerors through him that loved us" (Rom. 8:37, KJV)—your automatic response will be, "Not me."

When you hear the gospel message that says God loves you and has a great plan for your life, your "clogged filter" will respond, "Not me." Unless you get your mind back, cleansed from all that clogs it from the past, you cannot walk into your future in God. Only time spent in His presence will release God's truths into your spirit that will set you free from your past. If you sincerely want to be free and have your mind cleansed of wrong attitudes that keep you from walking in God's truth, why not pray this simple prayer right now?

> *Father, help me to see myself in the pages of this book. My heart is open. My spirit is open. I pray that You will help me confront the issues of my past and restore love and laughter, peace and joy to my life as I yield to the power of Your Holy Spirit. I pray that healing and wholeness would begin to be released in my life at this very moment. In Jesus's name, amen.*

GET YOUR FAITH BACK

Getting your faith back does not mean that you have lost your salvation or your faith. It means that other forces working within you or coming against you have prevailed in your life. You have given in to doubt, unbelief, or fear and need to deepen your relationship with God in order to face the future in faith once again.

The Bible declares that without faith it is impossible to please God (Heb. 11:6). It also teaches that God has given to every man a measure of faith (Rom. 12:3). So, when the enemy of your soul tries to convince you that you are hopeless because you do not have faith, declare the truth: "God has given me a measure of faith." God does not demand from us anything that He does not provide to us.

Faith is necessary to deepen your relationship with God, so it is important to understand what faith is. Entire books are written to discuss all the facets of personal faith in God. Here we can only describe the basic concept of faith as taught in the Scriptures:

> What is faith? It is the confident assurance that what we hope for is going to happen. It is the evidence of things we cannot yet see.
>
> —HEBREWS 11:1

Some have misunderstood faith, thinking it is based on a legalistic mental process of asserting that certain facts are true. So, they think that if you don't get what you believe God for, it is because you did not have enough faith. Others think that receiving from God through faith is only for the bold, the courageous. They feel like you can't truly be a person of faith until you conquer all of your intimidation and fears.

I have to confess that for a long time, the Bible's definition of faith left me confused. You see, a whole lot of things that I had faith for didn't happen. I believed God was going to heal my mother when she was ill. She died. I believed the house I had up for sale was going to be sold before the closing on the new one. It wasn't. As a result, I paid two mortgages for eight months. I believed that my son would give his heart to God when he was a teenager. He didn't. And so on, and so on.

> *Ultimately, developing a deeper relationship with God will result in a stronger marriage.*

There were other times I didn't believe I had faith because emotionally I didn't feel strong and powerful enough in a crisis situation. As a matter of fact, sometimes I just felt completely overwhelmed and helpless. Can you relate?

Undoubtedly, we are all faced with doubt and indecision at times and wonder how life situations relate to our faith in God. Have you ever asked, "Where is God in all this?" I have. In those moments, it is comforting to recall that many people in the Bible, whom we consider pillars of faith, had moments of doubt as they faced life's challenges. Abraham, Job, David, John the Baptist, and others faced crises in life that exposed their doubt.

Can you relate to John's poignant question to the Lord? "Are you really the Messiah we've been waiting for, or should we keep looking for someone else?" (Matt. 11:3). I can. In times when life throws you a curve and brings the unexpected crashing into your circumstances, it is natural to ask questions that reflect doubt in God's goodness, faithfulness, or power. That is why we must consistently seek God to cultivate our relationship with Him. Then, in those unexplainable times of overwhelming trouble, we can lean on Him, confident in His love for us in spite of the crisis we are experiencing.

REWARDED FOR FAITH

Have you realized that the people listed in the "hall of faith" (Heb. 11) all received God's approval because of their faith, without receiving that which God had promised? Why? This scripture gives us the answer:

> All of these people we have mentioned received God's approval because of their faith, yet none of them received all that God had promised. For God had far better things in mind for us that would also benefit them, for they can't receive the prize at the end of the race until we finish the race.
>
> —HEBREWS 11:39–40

The emphasis on receiving by faith what we desire cannot be based only on our temporal concerns of today. There is an eternal aspect of our journey as believers, and the race isn't over yet. It is obvious from the Scriptures that our faith is the object of God's delight. The apostle Peter said that the purpose of trials was to test our faith, to purify it as gold. He said that our faith was far more precious to God than mere gold (1 Pet. 1:7). Did he learn that from Jesus when He said to Peter, "I have pleaded in prayer for you, Simon, that your faith should not fail" (Luke 22:31)? I wonder.

God puts a premium on your faith, and He expects it to grow to maturity as you deepen your relationship with Him. Every believer is living at a different level of spiritual maturity. That's why it is so essential to become consistently involved in a local church, a functioning part of the body of Christ. The Bible says that God gave gifts to the church—apostles, prophets, pastors, and teachers—for the purpose of equipping God's people to do His work and to bring us to spiritual maturity and unity in our faith until we become like Christ (Eph. 4:11–13).

God gave us responsibility to look out for each other as well:

> Look after each other so that none of you will miss out on the special favor of God. Watch out that no bitter root of unbelief rises up among you, for whenever it springs up, many are corrupted by its poison.
>
> —HEBREWS 12:15

In a community of faith, you will learn to exercise your faith and to help the faith of others. You will be trained in the Word and equipped for the battle to help you overcome the battles and the lies with which the enemy tries to defeat you. God never meant for you to walk alone through life. He provided the church, His body, for instruction, spiritual guidance, encouragement, and united purpose to establish the kingdom of God in the earth.

To presume that you will get whatever you desire just because you believe God for it, unless it has its foundation in the Word of God, is a setup for potential disappointment, or worse—deception. So, faith must join hands with prayer, God's Word, and a mature understanding of God's will. My premise is that I'm going to believe God for the impossible while at the same time meditating and seeking to please Him. If I don't receive what I've prayed for, I am certain the Father knows what is best for me.

I love the apostle Paul's declaration as translated in the Amplified Bible: "For I consider that the sufferings of this present time (this present life) are not worth being compared with the glory that is about to be revealed to us and in us and for us and conferred on us!" (Rom. 8:18).

What's astonishing to me is that many of the prayers I prayed, which seemingly went unanswered, eventually turned out "exceedingly abundantly" better than I had

God puts a premium on your faith, and He expects it to grow to maturity

even thought to ask (Eph. 3:20, NKJV). To use a baseball analogy, it was as if I asked for a base hit, and the Father let me hit a grand-slam home run! As I have learned of His generosity, I have peace to wait for the expectations I haven't seen fulfilled yet. God continually gives me grace to stand in faith on His promises, and that's more than enough for me.

Don't let your emotions get the best of you. Don't let doubt overcome you in times of distress. Learn to share your problems with godly leaders and spiritual friends in the body of Christ to receive encouragement and guidance. And remember, the race isn't finished yet; there are eternal rewards awaiting you for your faith in God.

Meanwhile, watch out for the faith traps that presumption can lead you into. These tools of the enemy result in grave disappointment and even falling away from the faith if your prayer isn't answered exactly as you prayed it. Consider these dangers to your faith:

Hype-driven faith trap

Emotional desires make you declare something because you want it to be. These prayers have no biblical basis. They are based in self-centered, wishful thinking. God cannot be a partner in this presumptuous thinking or praying. Jesus said we must abide in Him and in His Word; then we can ask what we want, and it will be granted (John 15:6–7).

Double-minded faith trap

This trap is characterized by not consistently seeking truth. It is chasing after teachings and revelations that you can agree with and that make you feel good, preferring "truth" that agrees with your point of view. The apostle James said that a doubled-minded man is unstable in all his ways and cannot expect to receive anything from the Lord (James 1:7).

Fragmented faith trap

This trap includes fragmented families and fragmented churches. There are people who constantly try to go it alone, independently of the body of Christ. People who are willfully separated from other believers don't enjoy the full force of God's favor or the protection of His wisdom resident in mature believers. Jesus taught that there is great power in agreement even between two believers who are rightly related to the church (Matt. 18:15–20).

I believe the faith life can be summed up in Paul's words to Timothy: "For God has not given us a spirit of fear and timidity, but of power, love, and self-discipline" (2 Tim. 1:7). What a wonderful perspective on life. These are the things that make up a healthy attitude in the face of all of life's challenges:

- Divine power—authority and boldness to defeat every enemy
- Divine love—for ourselves and for others, reaching out in caring and effective ministry
- Sound mind—self-control, self-discipline, resulting in godly character

In short, deepening your relationship with God is the journey of life that will result in becoming transformed more and more into the image of Christ. I love the revelation that one hero of faith shares of her personal journey toward God:

> Most of the verses written about praise in God's Word were voiced by people faced with crushing heartaches, injustice, treachery, slander, and scores of other difficult situations. You don't have to be alone in your hurt! Comfort is yours. Joy is an option. And it's all been made possible by your Savior. He went without comfort so you might have it. He postponed joy so you might share in it. He willingly chose isolation so you might never be alone in your hurt and sorrow. The best we can hope for in this life is a knothole peek at the shining realities ahead. Yet a glimpse is enough. It's enough to convince our hearts that whatever sufferings and sorrows currently assail us aren't worthy of comparison to that which waits over the horizon.[2]
>
> —JONI EARECKSON TADA

What will your journey toward God require? He wants you to love Him with all your mind, your heart, and your strength. Whatever the cost of deepening your relationship with God and following Him with all your heart, the reward will far outweigh any sense of loss or sacrifice. The fulfill-ment of discovering your true purpose and destiny in this life will pay dividends you cannot imagine. As you discover your God-given passion, He will empower you to fulfill your goals and live your dreams.

Sometimes, continuing to fulfill divine destiny will require a new level of faith. After all, our faith is supposed to be growing like a grain of mustard seed, maturing and increasing its outreach and effectiveness. It may be that your life's passion seems lagging because it is time to be enlarged, to reach higher goals and greater achievements in the kingdom of God.

MAKING IT PERSONAL

The life of a Christian is not exempt from tragedy. How do you typically cope when tragedy strikes?

Does persistent worry replace persistent prayer in your life? If your answer is yes, write a prayer that asks God to help you abandon worry for prayer and get your prayer life back.

What do you need to rearrange or manage better to make prayer an effective part of your everyday life?

Unrepented sin can steal your joy. Destructive thought patterns, behavior, bitterness, and emotional wounds from the past can keep you from becoming whole. If this is your problem, I invite you to pray this prayer:

Father, I receive You wholly into my life. I need You to help me to deal with and overcome the things of the past and the present that have kept me from being the person You created me to be. Renew my mind. Restore me and fill me with the power of Your Spirit. Give me greater understanding and wisdom as I grow in Your love. As I prepare to pursue my passion, thank You for being my guide, my Father, and my friend.

CHAPTER 5

NEXT-LEVEL BELIEF

MORE THAN FIFTY THOUSAND people filled the Nelson Mandela Stadium in Namboole, Uganda. Thousands more waited outside the stadium, unable to get in, in spite of being soaked by the pouring rain as they pressed forward, hoping to attend this one-night worship experience. It was the biggest personal concert of my musical career. I could only wonder at the open door God had given me to minister to this vast audience of Ugandans.

Before the concert began, I had the privilege of meeting the first lady of Uganda, Janet Museveni, who, along with her security and other entourage of dignitaries, had come to share in this monumental musical event. An African choir made up of hundreds of voices enthusiastically sang to begin the concert, as the masses of people moved to the beat. Our host for the event, Pastor Robert Kayanja, eventually took the stage and, after greetings, began to share his heart about how important this event was to his nation.

You may remember that Uganda made headlines in the late 1970s and early 1980s because of its notorious dictator, Idi Amin. Unfortunately, when my generation thinks of this African nation, horrible pictures of murder and mayhem come to mind. It was common to read headlines during

Amin's rule of the brutality and murder of thousands of his own people, ordered by Amin himself.

Although Idi Amin is no longer in power, Uganda today is still facing a long, hard road of rebuilding their infrastructure and economy to secure a prosperous future for the beautiful people of Uganda. Rampant disease, witchcraft, poverty, and terrorism are just a few of the battles raging in their land that threaten the well-being of their citizens.

As I sat on that platform, listening to Pastor Kayanja address this great audience, I began to feel queasy in the pit of my stomach. Although at this point in my ministry I had sung on many great stages around the world, ministering at times with some dynamic, international speakers and evangelists, this anxious uneasiness persisted. Suddenly, as I sat there contemplating the incredible needs apparent in that vast audience, I felt woefully inadequate for the task at hand. I struggled to muster the faith I needed to minister to the people and feel that I could make a difference.

You see, in my mind, I was just a singer. Not a preacher. No healing ministry to speak of. No feeding program. Not a medical missionary or a person of influence in the political arena. I didn't have millions of dollars at my disposal to donate for the schools or hospitals they so desperately needed. I was just…a singer.

I found my thoughts evaluating my own life in light of what I was witnessing here. When I travel internationally to minister, I sing a few songs, say a few words of encouragement, and then go back home. Home—where the food is always good, the bed is nice and warm, the TV remote is never far away, and, above all, my family's safety is more secure than for multitudes in other nations. At home—my comfort zone.

Now, I was facing a massive audience of thousands of beautiful Ugandans who needed more than a few songs and a few words of encouragement. They needed God to invade their lives in a powerful way. They needed understanding and revelation of His great love for them. They needed healing—physical, emotional, and spiritual. I wasn't sure my faith level could touch God for those kinds of needs, even for one, much less for fifty thousand people.

It seemed, in those moments before I was introduced as the honored guest, that my belief in my God-given passion had taken flight and left the huge arena. All my confidence in my ability to make a difference seemed to vanish. What could I sing? What words could I say that would leave a lasting impact on the lives of the people? That would make a difference for their future? For eternity? It became clear in that situation that I needed a *new belief level*.

In my little moment of temporary insanity, I should have remembered the transforming power that the Word of God has when spoken over a life, when declared over someone's future. I forgot that I was singing about the wonderful, supernatural grace of God, to which I had been deeply committed all of my life. I had believed that the gospel of Christ is the power of God unto salvation. Hadn't it transformed my life and my family's life? Hadn't it helped us literally to *reinvent our lives*?

Yet, sometimes at home we get caught up in "having church," jumping and shouting, and expressing emotion without connecting to the powerful reality of the Christ of the gospel. Don't we? We forget that our message is a message of divine love and supernatural empowerment, of having a renewed mind and focus. It's a message of hope that goes way beyond temporal things; it ascends to higher realms of things eternal. Our message is the power of Jesus's name—it is definitely not about me.

In those anxious moments sitting on that platform, I should have realized that my belief is based on the principles and promises of God, whether I feel it or not. I needed to be grounded in my belief in God's faithfulness and what He called me to do, not just in my ability or experience. At the time, I was so focused on my

They needed God to invade their lives in a powerful way.

perceived inadequacies that I was almost overwhelmed. Yet, God proved His faithfulness once again, which resulted in my reaching out to a new level of belief.

In spite of my momentary lapse in faith-filled thinking, God revealed His love and power to the people that evening. As I sang His praises, He met us in a powerful and supernatural way. The people were spiritually hungry for the reality of God's love, and He satisfied their hearts with His saving presence. God will always meet you at the point of your need when you have faith to call out to Him.

Perhaps it was that faith of the people that ushered in God's presence. Perhaps it was the great mercy and compassion He displayed when He walked in Galilee and was moved by the needs of the multitudes. Whatever the catalyst, the supernatural power of God was released in that great arena that night, and through it all, it seemed as if my faith had reached out to a new level. A greater sense of God's heart filled me with desire to see God truly bless and empower His people.

FAITH FOR GREATER VICTORIES

Our journey to courage parallels the development of our capacity for new levels of faith. In short, it takes courage to believe for greater victories, and it takes greater faith to muster the courage to overcome bigger obstacles. Why do people achieve some measure of success in their walk with God and then seem to level out, live a predictable life, and display little hope of achieving their real dreams, their life passion?

For example, some people repeatedly find themselves in unhealthy relationships. They may leave one behind only to discover that their next relationship is just as unhealthy. Why? Because the low self-esteem they suffer does not allow them to see themselves in relationship with someone who truly cares about them and treats them with respect and dignity.

There are others who can never see themselves as intelligent people, capable of making independent decisions and choices for their lives. So, they're always looking to someone else to make the tough calls for their lives. Still others view all of life out of the dark lenses of negativity. They don't understand that adversity represents an opportunity to those who embrace it and search for the good that can come from it.

It is simply a fact of life that the quality of your life and the success you enjoy depends on how you see yourself. That is why it is so important to embrace the principles we have discussed about discovering your life's passion, deepening your relationship with God, and facing your fears and the lies that keep you from fulfilling your destiny in God.

Then, as you live to serve the purposes of God that He ordained for you, your faith will give you the courage to overcome even greater challenges. As you continue to grow throughout life in your dependency on God, you will see His faithfulness in ways you never dreamed.

In my wildest dreams, I could not have imagined ministering to that vast audience in Uganda and experiencing the power of God fill that arena as He did that night. I can only bow my heart in worship and deep gratitude for the journey to courage and a higher level of faith than I had experienced before. These are some of the lessons I learned to enter into a new level of belief for the impossible as God's servant.

HUMILITY LEADS THE WAY

It is truly humbling to be used by God in supernaturally powerful ways to bless people and release the power of God into their lives, especially when we realize where we came from and the problems He has saved us from in our own lives. Yet, it is that humility that leads the way to deeper relationship with God and new levels of belief in His goodness and faithfulness.

> *God will always meet you at the point of your need when you have faith to call out to Him.*

I remember talking to a good friend of mine years ago who was also a musician. His life was filled with difficulty at the time, trying to make a living as a musician. As a result, he and his family were struggling financially. I told him that during my years of struggling as a musician with a young family, I drove a taxicab for a few months to earn extra income. (It was not my favorite job; no offense to cab drivers.)

Also on my résumé were jobs I had pursued to supplement my singing career, including selling home security systems, life insurance, and panty hose (you read right!). Then there were the sales of magazine subscriptions, carpet, and a long list of other sales jobs, all meant to facilitate my flexible schedule needed as a professional Christian musician. I also told my friend that even now, having enjoyed years of financial success as a singer and songwriter, I am building side businesses unrelated to music.

My friend was not impressed with lessons of my painful journey. He retorted, "Well, I went to college to study music, and I'm not driving a cab or doing anything else but working in music!" I responded kindly, "I understand. Point taken." I did understand—only too well. He only saw himself as a musician. He could not function apart from his "identity," even though his family needed him as a husband, father, and provider. The memory of my family suffering the same economic woes as his still haunted me at times.

Reality dictated that, besides being a trained musician, my friend was also a husband, father, rent payer, auto-loan payer, school-supplies purchaser, grocery and clothing buyer—you get the picture. While I understood where he was coming from, I'm just not sure the wife, the kids, the landlord, the finance company, and Wal-Mart understood. I prayed for grace for him to humble himself and ask God to show him the way out of his dilemma.

When we are caught in the pride of our education, job title, or other "identity," it becomes difficult to face reality and realize that our priorities are skewed. When I aspired to be a Christian musician, the priority of my family's needs went unheeded. I had to face the music and understand that I was more than a musician; I was the head of a home and had responsibilities to fulfill that role as well.

One-dimensional people hinder true creativity at best and

lack problem-solving skills at worst. Seeking to find God's perspective for your identity is humbling, but it releases faith into your heart to receive His loving answer and supernatural intervention, and to embrace a larger image of yourself and your personal destiny.

The creation of solutions to problems is endless when we tap into next-level belief. That requires, first of all, that we humble ourselves and acknowledge our need to be responsible in every sphere of life to which we have been called.

FAITH VISUALIZES THE GOAL

When you embrace a posture of humility before the Lord, you will be able to exercise the next key to next-level belief. In order to move into another level of faith for your destiny, the first step you must take is to visualize that goal. That means receiving clarity about who you are, what God wants you to become, and where He wants you to be. Visualizing your goal is more than just daydreaming. Daydreaming is fantasizing about a wish without a plan in place to ever make it happen.

In contrast, when you look with the eyes of faith to fulfill what God has placed in your heart as your life passion, you can count on His supernatural intervention to make it happen. When you rehearse your vision in your mind over and over, prayerfully putting a plan in place to go forward, you will recognize the open door leading to what you've believed for. That's next-level belief.

The importance of having clear vision cannot be overstated. When Jesus asked His disciples who men thought He was, they responded that they had heard several opinions. Some thought He was John the Baptist, and some said Elijah. Others thought He was Jeremiah or another prophet.

Then Jesus asked them who they thought He was. Peter answered firmly, "You are the Messiah, the Son of the living God" (Matt. 16:16). He showed clarity of vision filled with revelation in his recognition of the Messiah. Jesus acknowledged that Peter had received that revelation from the Father (v. 17). Peter's revelation took him to a deeper level of belief as he chose to follow Christ, the Messiah. Because he saw Christ with eyes of revelation, even though he denied Him, Peter later preached that great sermon on the Day of Pentecost and became a strong leader of the early church.

Visualizing is not just understanding with your mind or seeing with your eyes. It involves revelation to your heart and spirit of what God has ordained for you. It requires growing and maturing in your relationship with God as you consistently seek to know Him. As a loving heavenly Father, God will be faithful to guide you into your destiny as you choose to walk with Him and become a mature son or daughter.

The godly responsibility of wise parents is to love, discipline, and educate their children until they become adults. But no matter how much we love them, one day our children must learn to take responsibility for their own lives. They will have to make their own choices and decisions and be responsible for their personal walk with God. No parent can fulfill the destiny of their child. That is a personal choice for every individual.

We all try to keep our babies little and cuddly as long as possible. We decry the day when we don't hear those baby sounds and watch that toddler running around discovering the world at our feet. But the reality is that a thirty-five-year-old baby isn't cute. It is so important that we see the potential in our children and affirm them in their journey to maturity.

When my son was two, I recognized him as a baby. When he was sixteen, I hailed him as a teenager. Now that he's an adult, I respect him as a man, a husband, and a father. As my son was my first child, it was difficult to recognize that the boy was no longer and the man was here to stay. Letting go was one of the hardest things for me to do. Yet, if I had not chosen to respect my son as a man capable of fulfilling his own destiny, I'd probably still be meddling in his life and treating him like he was a kid. To become a healthy-minded, mature man, he has to visualize his own destiny.

> *Seeking to find God's perspective for your identity is humbling*

RENEWING YOUR MIND

I believe the biggest battle we face today is a psychological assault on our beliefs. Media, religion, big business, sports, fashion gurus, politicians—it seems everyone is fighting for a chunk of our psychological "real estate." The way we view ourselves and others and whether we choose to act on what we believe will determine the destiny of our own life, our families, our nation, and, ultimately, our world.

You are held captive or set free by what you believe. You'll never change your life until you change what you believe. You will never change what you do until you change what you believe. The major factor for where you are today, in comparison with where you were last year, is what you have believed. The Bible is clear in its instruction about how we are to think. The apostle Paul taught:

> Don't copy the behavior and customs of this world, but
> let God transform you into a new person by changing
> the way you think. Then you will know what God wants
> you to do, and you will know how good and pleasing
> and perfect his will really is.
>
> —ROMANS 12:2

I once heard a pastor from Ghana say that Africans pray more than any other people group on the earth. Thousands of people gather together for all-night prayer meetings and call on God for hours at a time. Yet, Ghana is still one of the poorest nations. Why? Because prayer alone doesn't change you. What you believe changes you. Your mind-set will determine what you do with your faith, putting action to faith to bring results. If you line up your prayer with what you believe, you access the power to create change.

What you believe about God is not the only key to your success. You have to believe God's truth about yourself. Your mind has to be renewed to believe His love for you and that He has a divine purpose for your life. When you go through a divorce or financial failure, or you've just blown it, your biggest problem may not be your lack of belief in God. It could be that you no longer believe in yourself.

If you visualize yourself as a loser and a failure, as I viewed myself at one time, you will live out that "faith." We were not designed to get stuck in a defeated mind-set. Neither should we be comfortable not challenging who and what we believe. God never expected us to enter the church building and check our brains at the door. He won't get nervous if you evaluate who you are and where you are going. God accepts the challenge. Your doubts can help you press into God for the truth, which He will be faithful to reveal to you. His promise to every sincere believer is:

> You will seek me and find me when you seek me with all of your heart.
>
> —JEREMIAH 29:13, NIV

When you truly find out who God is, you find out who you are. And He has a lot to say about you. You are the beloved of God, fearfully and wonderfully made. You are a generation chosen to make known the purpose, power, and presence of God. The confidence we have is that

> *I believe the biggest battle we face today is a psychological assault on our beliefs.*

He didn't leave us here to fend for ourselves. He sent His Spirit to reveal Jesus to us, in us, and through us to others. In order to properly visualize your destiny, you will have to let your mind be renewed by God's Word.

GOD CONFIRMS HIS VISION

After seeking God and visualizing your goal, the second step to next-level belief is receiving confirmation from God in your spirit. As your heart becomes one with the heart and mind of God, your faith will be established in taking the steps you need to take to walk in the belief level. That is what I call God's will becoming your will.

It is also important to let other godly people in your life give counsel and help you confirm the vision God has given you. Again, it was Solomon, the wisest man who lived, who said, "With many counselors, there is safety" (Prov. 11:14).

Your pastor, mentor, or godly friend who has your best interests at heart can help confirm for you what God is saying to your heart. Sometimes, there is a need for wise timing, further training, or other steps to help you reach your goal successfully.

I have shared openly how, in my journey to courage and destiny, I felt completely inadequate to be used of God to bless anyone's life. Even when I was singing for people, I had trouble believing that God was making me an effective minister. Yet, as I sought God's will for my life, the desire to sing grew stronger, and I took steps to walk in that path toward music ministry. Slowly God began to confirm to my heart that I was walking in His vision for my life. He graciously used other people to confirm that God was touching their lives through my music ministry.

Now I love reading the comments that people enter on my website at www.alvinslaughter.com. Some have watched me sing on the Trinity Broadcasting Network. Others have heard one of my CDs or attended one of my concerts. They confirm the work of God in my heart to be a blessing and encourage me to reach for greater levels of faith. They remind me that I can still be effective even when I feel I've blown it. These friends helped to confirm to my heart what God has called me to do:

> Last year, I was listening to you sing "God Can Do Anything" when I was involved in a rollover automobile accident. I walked away without any injuries, and my car was totaled. That song has become my theme song, and I preach and teach it everywhere I go.
>
> —D. Woods

I just want to tell you how much I am enjoying your new CD, *The Faith Life*. It touches my heart very deeply. I find myself reaching out to the world spreading LOVE to everyone in need and praying that they are feeling what I'm feeling. PRAISE GOD! Keep doing the good work and reaching out to the world.

—V. VENABLE

Wow! I thank God for your inspirational life and music. I used to be so ashamed to sing in front of people, as I was shy. But once I watched your videos, you inspired me, and I want to express my love for God as you are doing. Thank you, Alvin. God bless you and your ministry.

—M. VAKACAVU

TAKING ACTION TO REALIZE YOUR VISION

When I finally realized that God was using me through music ministry to impact lives for His kingdom, I still limited Him in my faith to being a blessing to my local church family. But as I sought Him and found courage to walk through open doors, my mind kept expanding to grasp His vision for my life and ministry. I learned that the third step to next-level belief is to create it with your actions. Take small steps or big steps—it doesn't matter. Just get moving and begin creating momentum.

Eventually, I started believing for what seemed impossible to me. I embraced the truth that with God everything is possible. Before Uganda, I had ministered to other nations and had seen God bless the people. But in Uganda, sitting before that great audience and feeling suddenly inadequate to bring His presence to such needy people, I had to call on God to increase my faith.

My ministry in Uganda was an impetus for my next-level belief. I had first visualized ministering in the nations and said yes to the Spirit, who had confirmed that goal. Yet, if I had not taken action and walked through open doors, I would not have enjoyed the fulfillment of that goal of ministering to the nations.

Prayer alone doesn't change you. What you believe changes you.

In His great faithfulness, God saw my humility and heard my cry. He blessed my ministry there to build the kingdom of God, inspire others to build the kingdom of God, and to make Jesus famous. Not only is my music ministry accepted there, but also God connected me with a ministry in Africa to train up leaders to stem the tide of poverty and disease in their own nation. There truly is no limit to what God will do when we seek His passion for our lives.

It all began with humbling myself to visualize who God says I am. I'm not here to fit industry standards. I'm not here to blend in, but I am here to be a blessing. I'm a grown man and I'm my own man. I'm not looking for anyone's approval but the Father's, to love as He would have me to love, in the way He would have me do it.

God is continually renewing my mind through His Word and through prayer. As He does, He confirms His will for my life, my family, and my ministry. He expects me to follow that up with appropriate actions to achieve His goal for my destiny. I understand more and more that my journey toward fulfilling destiny requires that I believe—and keep on believing. I wrote a song called "I Believe" that expresses the lifelong spiritual posture that will be rewarded by fulfilling your God-given passion. (See Appendix A.)

As you determine to make it personal, I have outlined these steps to fulfilling your destiny in God. I encourage you to evaluate them in light of your own heart desires and prayerfully consider how to embrace them for your life.

MAKING IT PERSONAL

Think about the three steps to realizing your passion and walking in your divine destiny. List specific ways you will make them your own.

| |
| |
| |

Visualize your passion. What is your goal? Write down how or where you see yourself twelve months from now.

| |
| |
| |

Let it be confirmed in your spirit by the Word and through other godly friends. Write down what you commit to do every day to feed your spirit and connect with God until you hear that your will agrees with His. Allow Him to connect you with godly counselors.

| |
| |
| |

Create it with your actions. What is your plan, and what steps are you going to take? As you write them down, be specific and put a timetable on when you are going to take these actions. Continue to seek God for open doors to take even small steps toward fulfilling your passion.

| |
| |
| |

CHAPTER 6

GET GOING!

P ROCRASTINATION IS A TERRIBLE, and very common, human tendency to create delay in taking action. It can kill your future. To *procrastinate* simply means "to put off intentionally and habitually something that needs to be done." Where passion is concerned, while it is necessary to wait on God, as we discussed, it is ultimately your responsibility to *get going* when He gives direction for your life.

At the end of the last chapter, we discussed the importance of taking steps to move toward your goal. One of the greatest obstacles to action is procrastination. Now that you know where you are going and are seeing how to begin moving toward your destiny, you may encounter an unwillingness to move. That is procrastinating, putting off intentionally something that needs to be done.

So common is the fallacy of procrastination that you can find hundreds of famous quotes about it by just Googling the word. Here are a few quotes to help you think about how procrastination affects your life:

> You may delay, but time will not, and lost time is never found again.[1]
>
> —BENJAMIN FRANKLIN

Procrastination is one of the most common and dead-liest of diseases, and its toll on success and happiness is heavy.[2]

—WAYNE GRETZKY

We shall never have more time. We have, and have always had, all the time there is. Concentrate on something useful. Having decided to achieve a task, achieve it at all costs.[3]

—ARNOLD BENNETT

The secret of getting ahead is getting started.[4]

—MARK TWAIN

For years I've thought about writing this book. As a matter of fact, a publisher approached me a few years ago to discuss the prospects of writing a book. Even though I had been scratching my thoughts, ideas, and experiences on pieces of paper, recording them on my laptop and PDA for years, I showed my typical lack of self-belief by telling him, "I don't feel I have anything to say." I had not visualized myself as an author.

One of the greatest obstacles to action is procrastination.

Then, one day I was having lunch with David, a pastor friend, who was in the process of writing his next book. As a published author, he understood the time-consuming process, patience, and discipline required to write a book. In our conversation, I made the comment, "I could never write a book." When he asked me why not, I said something like, "I just can't. It's not my thing."

Pastor David looked thoughtfully down at his plate for

a moment. Then he made a statement that shook me into a rude awakening. "How sad it is that you have had so many experiences traveling the world, sharing the gospel in many different cultures, enjoying life-changing encounters, and meeting many important leaders, and all you have done is scratch notes to yourself. I believe others could benefit from the lessons of faith you have learned through those life encounters."

My jaw dropped as his words impacted me in that moment. I had never seen my life from that perspective before. Suddenly, I understood that when I'm long gone, my thoughts will go to the grave, and my scrap papers will be lost in a box in the attic or thrown out with the trash. Lessons learned that could have been shared would be lost forever.

As we continued to talk, Pastor David saw right through my lame excuse and nailed the real issue for my not writing a book. He said that my problem was not that I couldn't write or had nothing to say but that I would not discipline myself to write. In putting off the task of organizing my thoughts on paper, I was focusing on whether all the effort involved would end up being a best seller. I was not thinking about sharing the goodness of God in my life to be an inspiration to others or of leaving a legacy, an inheritance of wisdom to my children and to my grandchildren.

In that encounter with a godly mentor, God confirmed His vision for me to write this book. I recognized I was being irresponsible at best and not being a good steward of the blessings that God had given to me. I understood how procrastination was driving me to put off something God had really given me a vision to do, which explained the hundreds of handwritten notes on scrap paper. I could relate to this insightful quote about the power of procrastination working in my life:

> Procrastination is the fear of success. People procrastinate because they are afraid of the success that they know will result if they move ahead now. Because success is heavy, carries a responsibility with it, it is much easier to procrastinate and live on the "someday I'll" philosophy.[5]
>
> —DENIS WAITLEY

So, here I am, creating a book to help inspire you to avoid the pitfalls of procrastination and other enemies to walking in your God-given destiny. And you know, surprisingly, I am actually enjoying the process. As I began to write, I even started thinking about other topics and books that I want to write about after finishing this one.

It is more amazing to me because when I was in school years ago, I hated writing. I love to talk. I love to sing. I love to laugh. And I love to eat, but I never dreamed I could love to write. Now, I have received so many encouraging replies to my blogs (www.alvinslaughter.net) and also on my Facebook page (www.facebook.com/alvinslaughterinternational) that I can now say that I love to write. More than that, I love the responses from my readers.

OUR PART IS TO KEEP MOVING

In all of life's pursuits, no matter how godly, we must be aware that not everything we do will result in fantastic success. We have to be willing not to meet our goals perfectly and even to fail at times in order to do our part just to keep going. That was the apostle Paul's attitude when he admitted that he had not arrived at perfection, but he was pressing toward the goal:

> I don't mean to say that I have already achieved these things or that I have already reached perfection! But I keep working toward that day when I will finally be all that Christ Jesus saved me for and wants me to be....I am focusing all my energies on this one thing: Forgetting the past and looking forward to what lies ahead, I strain to reach the end of the race and receive the prize for which God, through Christ Jesus, is calling us up to heaven.
>
> —Philippians 3:12–14

Most of us would agree that the apostle Paul was a fantastic success as a Christian and leader of the early church. Yet, his focus was on continuing the race to the end, not on what he had already accomplished. If you read his story, you will find times when he was discouraged and hindered in his goals by the devil. But Paul did his part—he just kept going.

Blessings in Disguise

What is interesting about our journey is that some of the pitfalls and interruptions along the way may in fact turn out to be blessings in disguise. Consider this analogy: You are a passenger on a plane to Chicago that is diverted to Philadelphia because of bad weather in Chicago. You miss your scheduled conference in Chicago. While stranded in Philly, you engage in a long conversation with a stranger who ends up eventually becoming a good friend, a business associate, or maybe even your spouse.

It is God's wonderful pleasure to work all things together for our good (Rom. 8:28). He can only do that when we are moving forward in His revealed will so that He has some "things" to work together. The fact is that not everything you hope for will happen, and some things you did not want to happen will. But even if the worst happens, God causes everything to work together for our good when we are walking in His purposes. Our part is to keep pressing toward our God-given goal.

Nine months after Jonathan White was married, a drunk driver ran a red light going ninety miles per hour and hit his parents' car. His father died instantly, and his mother lived for sixteen days in the hospital before she too went home to be with the Lord. After some time passed and grief was giving way to hope, Jonathan and his wife, Sheila, thought they were entering a brighter phase of life together.

During the year following his parents' deaths, this newly married couple found out that Sheila was pregnant. "We were so excited because we were thinking that this would help heal the hurt caused by losing my parents," said Jonathan. However, the doctors did not have good news for the Whites. They were informed soon after their daughter's birth that the baby had Down syndrome.

"At first, I was angry, thinking that God had given us second best," said Jonathan. "However, I have found that God knows exactly what He is doing, and He gave us the very best that He had. Our daughter, Brittany, has been a wonderful blessing to us and to many others who know her."[6] Theirs is a wonderful testimony that no person is born with less worth than another. It is simply a matter of learning to appreciate the precious gift of life expressed in every person.

Songwriter Bruce Carroll recorded a moving tribute called "Sometimes Miracles Hide" to a couple who had a baby born with Down syndrome.[7] (See Appendix B.) We have to recognize the miracles of life hidden in what otherwise might seem to be a disappointment. Life will sometimes present surprises, good or bad, that we have to embrace if we are to keep moving toward the goal of becoming all Christ wants us to be. We have to view every circumstance as subject to His sovereignty and determine to love Him through it all—and just keep moving.

Hidden within the process of getting started is the seed of blessing and empowerment to move toward our goal. If you wait for the perfect time and situation to get started, doing what you know is your heart's passion and becoming the person you want to be, you will wait forever. Nothing is ever perfect.

You are made in the image of the Creator, and though you are not God, you have an innate power to create. When you determine to create the destiny that God has placed in your heart, He works on your behalf. You create through careful preparation and focused activity. Then God works in His own time, opening every door that should be opened and closing every door that should be shut. In short, your getting started toward your goal can be reduced to this equation:

> *Our part is to keep pressing toward our God-given goal.*

PREPARATION + ACTIVITY + TIME = OPPORTUNITY

C. Northcote Parkinson, a famous British historian, wrote of procrastination, "Delay is the deadliest form of denial."[8]

How true! In procrastinating, we deceive ourselves into thinking we really are going to do something, someday, so we don't face the truth that we are really killing our future through denial. This creative action is not just about working hard to make a better life. It is about getting your power back; it is about using what you have in your hand to take you forward to limitless possibilities in fulfilling your passion.

It is this creative action that will attract true wealth into your life through the promises of God. True wealth is so much more than big cars and big houses. True wealth is having abundance in your life to give to others, spiritually first, then socially and economically. Jesus warned against greed for material things: "Watch out! Be on your guard against all kinds of greed; a man's life does not consist in the abundance of his possessions" (Luke 12:15, NIV).

When you learn the true value of life and have the freedom to become the godly person you were destined to become, to know the power of God, and to be able to touch other lives with His love, then you are living an abundant life.

> *Though you are not God, you have an innate power to create.*

As I have shared, one of life's most important lessons I have had to learn is to get over myself, to focus on helping others do the same by getting rid of the stuff that clogs our minds and keeps us from enjoying the presence and love of God.

I know the pain of living from paycheck to paycheck; it is a horrible way to exist. You're just one crisis away from losing everything. You suffer sleepless nights, living in constant fear that soon you'll be living on the streets. I also know the terrible pain of living with a broken heart. It is a deep, agonizing pain that reaches into the pit of your soul. You feel devastated...lost...powerless.

All this stuff clogs our minds and keeps us from moving toward destiny. As believers, to say that we know God but not be close enough to Him to get solutions and know the joy of serving Him is depressing. It is like spiritual and emotional quicksand! But the principles I am sharing in this book have worked in my life, and they will work in yours. I encourage you to study it again and prayerfully *get going*, so that you can see God begin to move supernaturally in your life and circumstances.

MAKING IT PERSONAL
Are you a procrastinator? Can you identify how procrastination has hindered you specifically from your life passion?
What steps can you take to *get going*?
What would "true wealth" in your life look like? How can you pursue it?
You are created in the image of God with an innate ability to create. What do you think you can create as you function in your passion?

CHAPTER 7

MAKING IT WORK FOR YOU

I F YOU HAVE READ to here, let me congratulate you. The truths you have read can work for you as they have for me and many other believers who dare to embrace them. Now, let me get extremely practical and leave you with seven keys to making these truths work in your life, empowering you to reach your ultimate destiny in God.

I challenge you to keep these principles close by as you seek God to discover your passion, deepen your relationship with God, and get started toward your newly confirmed life goals. No task is too daunting that helps you reach the ultimate goal. What would you do with your life if you didn't pursue your passion? Years wasted, opportunities squandered, frustration, disappointment, and depression are poor substitutes for the hard work of pursuing your passion. So, consider these ways to jump-start your transformation and determine to get going:

ANTICIPATE VICTORY

Failure is part of the process of life. Without experiencing the pang of failure, you probably have attempted little. But to live in constant fear of failure that keeps you from taking advantage of opportunities in life is self-defeating. Sometimes we never get going because we don't feel we can succeed. Every endeavor of life has its consequences, but you will never get your power back until you convince yourself and allow God to convince you that success, victory, and overcoming are possible—for you. Learn to cultivate an anticipation of victory, knowing that God always causes us to triumph:

> Now thanks be unto God, which always causeth us to triumph in Christ, and maketh manifest the savour of his knowledge by us in every place.
> —2 Corinthians 2:14, kjv

Begin With the End in Mind

Develop a blueprint for how you're going to get to the place in life you want to be. You don't need all the details, but you must become a visionary, not just a dreamer given to wishful thinking. Dreamers think about what they would like to become if only... Visionaries develop strategies to help them get there. Most of the time you'll have to tweak your strategy as you move toward your goal, because you will run into some roadblocks along the way. No problem. The more you strategize, the better you become at it.

Become a Student of Personal Development

Wait on God daily and read His Word, embrace His promises, and let the Holy Spirit help you to overcome fear—fear of failure and of people's opinions of you. Learn how to deal with rejection. Brush it off, and you will become a person of influence.

All of these victories are a result of personal development. Some people call it self-help or self-discovery. Call it what you want. It is God's work in you to transform your thinking, renewing your mind with His truth about yourself and your destiny. Your mind is the command center that will get you going in the right direction—God's.

For example, one of the reasons people don't lose weight is because they don't have a healthy self-image. The diet industry thrives on treating symptoms; it does not touch this root problem of low self-esteem. Allowing God to renew your mind will destroy the root of the problem and set you on a path to overcome obesity.

The same is true for people in bad marriages or other negative relationships. God will empower you to overcome every obstacle when you embrace His truths about yourself, your worth, and your divine destiny. No matter how heartbreaking your personal story, you can receive a miracle from God when you determine to embrace these principles and allow Him to work in your relationships. A powerful example of such a miracle is the story of our friend Linda, whose life seemed to be a desperate series of mistakes. Yet, God redeemed them and gave her a wonderful victory. (Please see Appendix D for her story.)

When we work on ourselves, we become less defensive and more patient and understanding. We begin to let go of the baggage that we bring to our relationships. One of the greatest sources of personal development for me is the principles found in the Bible books of John, Ephesians, and Romans.

Personal development is an ongoing process throughout life. Make it your mission, and take responsibility to continue to grow by being "transformed by the renewing of your mind.

Then you will be able to test and approve what God's will is—his good, pleasing and perfect will" (Rom. 12:2–3, NIV).

"SELL, SELL, AND SELL!"

You have to learn to sell in order to be an overcomer. Let me explain. I am not talking about becoming a salesman to earn a living. I am talking about promoting your God-given purpose so that others will buy into your victory and be inspired to pursue their own God-given passion. One prominent meaning of *sell* is "to cause to be accepted; to advocate successfully; to persuade (another) to recognize the worth or desirability of something."

> *Wait on God daily and read His Word.*

The first sale you must make is to yourself. I had to sell myself on the idea that I could be in music ministry full-time, as I shared earlier. I even had to sell myself on writing this book. Knowing there are thousands of books published every year, I had to sell myself on the fact that there are people who are going to pick up this book and find the encouragement they need to begin to change their lives.

You must learn how to sell, first of all, in order to get your power back. Promoting your passion is the most powerful antidote against rejection or fear of others' opinions. Instead of passively receiving those negative forces, which results in giving your power away to them, you are declaring your personal destiny. And God is empowering you to do so.

Consider how selling works in life. Nothing happens in life until a sale is made. Teens are always trying to sell their parents on their independence, asking, "Why can't I stay out until two a.m.? All my friends do." Parents are trying to sell their teens on their authority: "I want you home by midnight!" When you're on a first date or a job interview, you're selling the strength of your personality, character, skills, and abilities.

Churches and other charitable organizations must sell their members and donors on their need for continued financial support. A great preacher or public speaker must learn how to sell his ideas effectively if he or she wants to win their audience, persuading them to believe what they are teaching. (How am I doing?)

I suggest you aid your personal development by reading books written by experts who articulate principles on how to be an effective salesperson.

No Excuses

You can make excuses for not achieving your life passion, or you can live your life walking by faith in your destiny, but you can't do both. If you say, "I can," you're right. If you say, "I can't," you will live like you are also right. Choose to say, "I can," and then stick to it. The rewards are unimaginable. Don't let momentary setbacks become an excuse for accepting failure. Get up, dust yourself off, and start again!

Fence-Sitting Is Not an Option

Og Mandino, an American motivational author and speaker, said this about the fatal malady of indecision:

> To be always intending to make a new and better life but never to find time to set about it is as to put off eating and drinking and sleeping from one day to the next until you're dead.[1]

Your relationship with God cannot be put off as some half-hearted, religious attempt at serving Him. To get your power back and reinvent your life, you have to be vitally connected to God through Jesus Christ by the power of the Spirit, as we discussed in chapter 4.

When you seriously seek God as your priority in life, God goes before you and orders your steps. His will, His way—no exceptions. Jesus did nothing without first praying and seeking the will of the Father (John 5:30). Don't waste your life doing things your own way and then wonder where God is when it doesn't work.

I recorded a song called "The Faith Life," written by my friend Keith Laws. This song has a powerful message about launching out and letting your faith make you fly. (See Appendix C.) It is much more exhilarating to fly in faith than to fence-sit in failure.

GIVE IT AWAY

The primary truth about the power of giving is revealed to us as God the Father gave His only Son to save us:

> For God so loved the world, that he gave his only begotten Son, that whosoever believeth in him should not perish, but have everlasting life.
>
> —JOHN 3:16, KJV

God doesn't only bless us so that we can fulfill our passion and destiny. Inherent in everyone's God-given passion is the desire of the Father to give. He loves giving good things to His children. He wants us to give also. I don't believe I'll ever fully understand how increase comes into our lives when we give; I simply know by experience that it does. Jesus promised:

> If you give, you will receive. Your gift will return to you in full measure, pressed down, shaken together to make room for more, and running over. Whatever measure you use in giving—large or small—it will be used to measure what is given back to you.
>
> —LUKE 6:38

I am who I am in life today because God used His servants to give to me. Some gave hope and encouragement, others forgiveness and truth. Still others gave me their time and attention, their patience and understanding, love and laughter. Some even gave money and material possessions to meet material needs.

> *The first sale you must make is to yourself.*

Think about it. Whatever measure of success you are enjoying, you didn't get there solely by yourself. Gratitude for the people God uses to help us grow is a sign of maturity and godly humility. If you need to grow some more, as we all do, it will likely require someone God places into your path to help you on your journey.

Consider what you can receive of true wealth when you choose to give to others:

- If you're a patient person, give understanding. Get virtue back.

- If you're a joyful person, give laughter. Get pleasure back.

- If you're strong, give a hand. Get appreciation back.

- If you're enthusiastic, light somebody's fire. Get passion back.

- If you're a good listener, lend an ear. Get discernment back.

- If you're a talker, speak life. Get encouragement back.

- If you've been wronged, give forgiveness. Get your power back.

I can only think of six reasons that hinder giving. They are poverty, selfishness, mismanagement, uncaring, lack of faith, and being stingy. Even these are poor excuses for not giving. I challenge you to study the promises of God's Word regarding giving and to embrace the truths of generosity that will set you free to enjoy prosperity of heart, mind, and material possessions.

Gratitude for the people God uses to help us grow is a sign of maturity and godly humility.

When you give, you have the ability to greatly affect someone's life. In that way, giving makes you a powerful person. You can use your God-given abilities and resources to become someone's answer to prayer! There is no thing more powerful that reflects the image of Almighty God. That is priceless!

I hope you have benefited from the life principles shared in this book. They have worked for me, and I know they will work for you. So, I challenge you: dare to accept the challenge that God has placed before you and reap the wonderful reward of overcoming every obstacle, renewing your mind, conquering your fears, and living the abundant life Christ came to give to you.

I can testify that it is worth every step of the sometimes painful journey. The rewards far outweigh the rigors of the battle. Just knowing that God is with you to empower you to win against all odds is enough impetus to get you started on your quest for your life passion and to keep you going forward.

See you on the journey.

MAKING IT PERSONAL

List three ways you can anticipate victory.

As you begin with the end in mind, list what you want the end to be. Then write down steps that will begin your journey to that end.

Sell, sell, and sell! List three ways you can learn to sell your passion so that others can profit from your life in God.

EPILOGUE

W HEW! THIS YEAR HAS been like a roller-coaster ride for me. Yet, my faith has never been stronger. I've never been more determined. I have grown in my love for God and people. I'm still working on some other stuff, but we'll talk about that another time. All that means is that with God's great grace, I am still *reinventing life.*

If you've had a rough year, God is not mad at you. As a matter of fact, God loves you so much, He has already supplied all of your needs according to His riches in glory. No recession. No fear. No confusion. No delusion.

I absolutely refuse to participate in the recession! That means that I won't let the media's bad news about Wall Street dictate how I feel. To live is Christ; to die is gain (Phil. 1:21). I will not be afraid.

When fear threatens to attack me, I remember the first step I made to reinvent my life: *get clarity.* That comes from the presence of God as I seek Him in His Word and in prayer. I declare with the psalmist: "You will show me the way of life, granting me the joy of your presence and the pleasures of living with you forever" (Ps. 16:11).

The second step to reinventing life is to *live boldly.* Seek God for courage and boldness to throw off fear. He did not give you a spirit of fear or timidity, but of power, love, and self-discipline ("a sound mind," KJV) (2 Tim. 1:7).

Your part is to put the destiny God reveals to you in

motion. If you surrender your will and plans to God, He will move heaven and Earth to open every door that should be open and to close every door that should be shut. It is a constant adventure with God to see how He leads you into fulfillment of your passion. Cooperate with His plan, and He will reinvent your life.

What God may be doing is trying to get us to realize that we are imperfect people in an imperfect world. We make mistakes. We blow it BIG-TIME. We have all been guilty of living our lives based on our dysfunctions. That's why it's so important that we find our true identity through who God says we are rather than from our culture, a bad childhood, or a mentality of constantly berating ourselves. We have to let our minds be renewed through self-discipline, allowing the truth of God's Word to prevail in our thoughts.

We have the God-given ability to solve problems. "Jesus Will Work It Out" is a good song title, but some things He is not going to do for you. He gave you the power to work it out. How? By making right decisions, personally developing, learning, and growing in your faith. Only then can you have true prosperity. Your are blessed to be a blessing!

I believe in miracles and have seen them in my life. I believe God loves me, and He manifests His love to me daily. But I also know that I still have some tough decisions to make in the days ahead. Some things I have to determine to hold on to. Other things I have to let go. God Himself will give me the wisdom to know the difference and the strength to be firm and steadfast in the faith.

So this year, determine to get unstuck. Let God help you to reinvent your life. You must take biblical steps to get refreshed, get focused, and let your mind be transformed.

And keep at it. There is no substitute for perseverance in your walk with God.

Dare to develop the skills you need to bring overflow into your life. You see, God gave us incredible brainpower as well as access to His great power. Our God-given minds have developed some pretty amazing inventions. As a believer, don't limit His creativity residing in you. Let your faith make you fly! Enjoy the journey!

I look forward to seeing you along the way!

"I BELIEVE" *by Alvin Slaughter*

Know God is to love God

Love God is to serve God

Serve God is to believe in God

We must believe until the weary citizens of this generation find rest and peace for their soul

Believe until the brokenhearted find a balm for healing and forgiveness

Believe until the evil of prejudice is an ancient thing of our ignorant past

Believe until every wide-eyed, tender-hearted little boy and little girl really, really knows that, "yes, Jesus loves me"

Believe so that the cleansing blood of Christ will never be in vain

Believe until somebody...whosoever will...anybody can see the love of God in you and in me

Believe...and keep on believing

Believe until the whole wide world knows that yes, there is a more excellent way

And now abides faith, hope, and love...these three. But the greatest of these is love.[1]

"SOMETIMES MIRACLES HIDE" *by Bruce Carroll*

YEARS AGO, SONGWRITER BRUCE Carroll recorded a song about a couple he knew who had a child born with Down syndrome. The song is called, "Sometimes Miracles Hide." As you read these lyrics, let the beauty of God's gift of life fill your heart, and may you experience in your own life those "miracles that hide."

They were so excited it was coming to be,
Two people so in love and now soon there would be three.
For many years they planned it. Now soon it would be true.
She was picking out the pink clothes; he was looking at the
    blue.
The call came unexpected,
The doctor had bad news.
Some tests came back and things weren't right, said
    you're gonna have to choose, "I'll wait a week for your
    decision," and then the words cut like a knife,
"I'm sure everyone will understand if you want to end its
    life."
Though they were badly shaken they just had no choice,
Because they knew God creates no accidents and they were
    sure they heard His voice sayin'

Sometimes miracles hide,
And God will wrap some blessings in disguise, and you
may have to wait this lifetime to see the reasons with
your eyes, 'cause sometimes miracles hide.

It seemed before they knew it the appointed day arrived,
With eager apprehension they could barely hold inside.
The first time they laid eyes on her confirmed the doctors
fears,
But they held on to God promise, they were sure they both
could hear.

Sometimes miracles hide,
And God will wrap some blessings in disguise, and you
may have to wait this lifetime to see the reasons with
your eyes, 'cause sometimes miracles hide.

Though she was not like the other girls, they thought she
was the best,
And through all the years of struggle, neither whispered
one regret.
And the first day that she started school and took her first
bus ride,
They'd remembered the words that God had spoke, and
they both broke down and cried.
You see, to them it did not matter why some things in life
take place,
'cause they just knew the joy they felt when they'd look into
her face.

They learned that sometimes miracles hide.
They said God has wrapped our blessing in disguise, and
we may have to wait this lifetime to see the reasons with
our eyes.
We know sometimes miracles hide. We've learned
sometimes miracles hide.[1]

"THE FAITH LIFE" *by Keith Laws*

Sometimes we hold on a little longer than we should
Letting go can be hard, but it's sometimes for our good
The fear of what's ahead, sometimes makes us fall behind
You can see the times are changing
But pretend that you're so blind
You'll never really know just what the future holds
But we know, God holds us in His hand
So by faith, we must climb into the boat
And follow His command
Launch out into the deep
Let your faith take you somewhere
That you've never been before
Launch out into the deep
Let your faith make you fly, let your faith make you soar
Launch out, launch out into the deep
It's time to wake up, and make our dreams come true
Time is always moving, and it will not wait for you
The fear inside your mind, can quench the fire in your
    heart
Sometimes where you end, is where God wants to start
It's never easy when you're walking out by faith
Everything seems so different and new
But if we only learn to see with eyes of faith
We could see life in a different view
Launch out into the deep
Let your faith take you somewhere
That you've never been before

Launch out into the deep
Let your faith make you fly, let your faith make you soar
Launch out, launch out into the deep
So much for you awaiting
So stop procrastinating
Close your eyes,
Just take a leap
Launch out into the deep
Let your faith take you somewhere
That you've never been before
Launch out into the deep
Let your faith make you fly, let your faith make you soar
Launch out, launch out into the deep.[1]

LINDA'S STORY OF TRIUMPH

I HAVE A DEAR FRIEND whom I have known for over twenty years. To protect her identity, I'll call her Linda.

Linda was in an abusive marriage for many years, feeling trapped in that relationship as she tried to raise her children in New York City. She went to church regularly, sang in the choir, and was involved in outreach ministries. But any joy she felt in raising her children and serving God was erased by the emotional and physical abuse she suffered when her husband came home.

After a painful and emotionally draining divorce, she moved to upstate New York, trying to rebuild her life and escape the reminders of how her fairy-tale marriage had turned into such a horrible nightmare.

As time went by, and with her children all grown up, she met a handsome, kind, giving man at her place of employment. Based on appearances, he was just the kind of man she needed. They began a relationship, and everything went great, it seemed. Maybe a few little bumps in the road here and there, which was to be expected. It was nothing that could not be worked out.

Linda and her new friend married. On their wedding night, to Linda's dismay, her newly wed husband seemed transformed before her eyes. Horrified, she saw a personality she had never known, as he screamed curses at his new bride for no apparent reason. Linda was dazed but determined to make this marriage work. Yet, from that moment, she constantly lived under the fear of his ferocious outbursts and anger.

Before their marriage, they had agreed that, with her children grown, they would not have more children. That changed also. He forced her to quit her job and have more children. She bore him two sons, starting over again to raise their children. But things only got worse.

Linda's husband began to hit her, physically abusing her and verbally berating her in his angry tirades. Now unemployed with two young boys, Linda began to suffer financially as well. He would give her very little money to take care of the home and children. She was virtually a prisoner in her own home.

Then, her husband began having affairs with other women and dared her to try to leave or do anything about it. He made her to feel worthless. She felt helpless. Even if she looked for a job, who would hire her? How would she take care of the children?

Linda often thought of leaving him, but she could not face the thought of a second failed marriage and raising two boys alone. So, she turned to prayer. Maybe God would turn his heart. Maybe he would see the error of his ways. Maybe it was all her fault.

The final straw came when Linda's husband started bringing women home and having sex with them in their bed. Outraged, Linda took her boys and fled to her married daughter's home. She felt like she couldn't breathe. There she was, embarrassed, devastated, humiliated.

Linda had lived with this painful secret until she could

bear it no longer. She found refuge in my wife's ladies' prayer group. The prayers, support, and testimonies of the other women, some who had been through similar situations, strengthened Linda and helped her find her way.

Eventually, she found the courage to file for divorce. Destitute, with two boys to raise, she still told her attorney that she didn't want anything from him; she just wanted to see this chapter of her life closed. Linda told her attorney that she was a Christian and didn't want to fight anymore. Though she desperately needed financial help, she did not think her husband had much money anyway.

The attorney respected Linda's wishes but told her kindly that she would not tell Linda how to pray, and Linda was not to tell her how to practice law. She understood that for justice to be served, Linda would have to fight, and she was going to help her do that. You see, the truth is that at times in order to get your power back, to keep your faith strong, you have to fight.

The attorney went to work, and the proceedings went forward. When the attorney went inside the conference room to negotiate a settlement with the husband's attorneys, Linda sat outside the conference room, a bundle of nerves—praying.

After what seemed like forever, the negotiations came to an end. Linda looked up in time to watch her smiling attorney approaching her. She had learned that Linda's husband had hidden large sums of money from her during the marriage and that Linda was going to receive a large, five-figure lump-sum settlement along with monthly child support.

One week earlier, Linda was embarrassed that she couldn't afford to cash a twenty-five dollar check at the bank because she didn't have enough in her account to cover it. Now, she had enough to move out of her daughter's home, find a home of her own, and make a fresh start to raise her two little boys.

Throughout this crisis, Linda was learning valuable principles of overcoming her own weaknesses—facing the music, so to speak. She now realized that her low self-esteem, which drove her to feel she needed to have a companion in her life to make her feel worthy of love, was the catalyst that opened her to very abusive men. God had intervened and given her a wonderful miracle, not just financial, but of wholeness and destiny.

Now, just a couple of years later, Linda is successfully raising her sons. She works full-time for an international Christian missions organization. She's a leader in the women's prayer group and a head of the prayer and Bible study group at her church. Linda has also become a mentor to young girls and is a passionate soulwinner, sharing the love of Christ with everyone she meets. Hers is a wonderful story of someone who had lost her joy, her peace, her self-respect, and ultimately her sense of purpose—her passion.

God, in His great mercy, taught her the life principles she needed to make her a whole person, capable of healthy relationships, and able to discover her destiny. He wants to do the same for everyone who will call on His name and be willing to *reinvent life*.

NOTES

Chapter 1—Discovering Your Life's Passion

1. H-Net, "Mr. Polk's Other War," H-Net.org, http://www.h
-net.org/reviews/showrev.php?id=8192 (accessed November 11,
2009).

2. "James Knox Polk," Miller Center of Public Affairs, http://
millercenter.org/academic/americanpresident/polk/essays/biography/
print (accessed November 11, 2009).

3. Corrie ten Boom Museum, "History," CorrietenBoom.com,
http://www.corrietenboom.com/history.htm (accessed November 12,
2009).

Chapter 3—Confronting Failure Myths

1. "Nelson Mandela Quotes," ThinkExist.com, http://
thinkexist.com/quotation/there-is-no-passion-to-be-found-playing
-small-in/348626.html (accessed November 16, 2009).

2. Steven Berglas, *Success Syndrome* (Cambridge, MA: Da
Capo Press, 1986).

Chapter 4—Deepening Your Relationship With God

1. "Joni Eareckson Tada Story," JoniEarecksonTadaStory.com,
http://joniearecksontadastory.com/ (accessed November 16, 2009).

2. "Christian Quotes by Joni Eareckson Tada,"
DailyChristianQuote.com, http://dailychristianquote.com/dcqtada
.html (accessed November 17, 2009).

Chapter 6—Get Going!

1. "Benjamin Franklin Quotes," iWise.com, http://www.iwise
.com/pbYmB (accessed November 18, 2009).

2. "Wayne Gretzky Quotes," ThinkExist.com, http://
thinkexist.com/quotation/procrastination_is_one_of_the_most_
common_and/149962.html (accessed November 18, 2009).

3. "Procrastination Quotes," Quotespedia.com, http://my
-quotes-collection.blogspot.com/2008/02/procrastination-quotes
.html (accessed November 18, 2009).

4.   "Mark Twain Quotes," ThinkExist.com, http://thinkexist
.com/quotation/the_secret_of_getting_ahead_is_getting_
started/216812.html (accessed November 18, 2009).

5.   "Denis Waitley Quotes," ThinkExist.com, http://thinkexist
.com/quotation/procrastination_is_the_fear_of_success
-people/296563.html (accessed November 18, 2009).

6.   Jonathan White, "Biography," JonathanWhiteMusic.com,
http://www.jonathanwhitemusic.com/biography.php (accessed
November 19, 2009).

7.   Bruce Carroll, "Sometimes Miracles Hide," BruceCarroll
.com, http://www.brucecarroll.com/default.aspx?pid=88 (accessed
November 19, 2009).

8.   "C. Northcote Parkinson," ThinkExist.com, http://
thinkexist.com/quotation/delay_is_the_deadliest_form_of_
denial/253524.html (accessed November 19, 2009).

Chapter 7—Making It Work for You

1.   Og Mandino, "Laura Moncur's Motivational Quotations,"
http://www.quotationspage.com/quote/38193.html (accessed
November 19, 2009).

Appendix A—"I Believe" by Alvin Slaughter

1.   Alvin Slaughter, "I Believe," *On the Inside*, © 2003 by Alvin
Slaughter Music and Integrity Music, Inc. Permission applied for.
Available at www.itunes.com and www.worshipmusic.com, or call
Integrity Music at (251) 633-9000.

Appendix B—"Sometimes Miracles Hide" by Bruce Carroll

1.   Bruce Carroll, "Sometimes Miracles Hide," *Sometimes
Miracles Hide*, © 1991 by Word Music Group. Permission applied for.

Appendix C "The Faith Life" by Keith Laws

1.   Keith Laws, "The Faith Life," *The Faith Life* by Alvin
Slaughter, © 2005 by Integrity Music, Inc. Permission applied for.
Available at www.itunes.com or www.worshipmusic.com, or call
Integrity Music at (251) 633-9000.

RESOURCE PAGE

You may access more helpful information and contact the author of *Reinvent Your Life* at the following Web sites:

JOIN THE **OVERCOMERS!**

www.alvinslaughter.com—the official Web site of Alvin Slaughter, international recording artist, inspirational speaker, and OVERCOMER!

www.alvinslaughter.net—Alvin's Blog, where you can get help to reinvent YOUR life with ongoing instruction from Alvin Slaughter. Turn YOUR LIFE around, rediscover the fire of YOUR FAITH, and get YOUR POWER back!

JOIN THE **FUN!**

www.facebook.com/AlvinSlaughterInternational —interact with Alvin and thousands of friends on Facebook.

JOIN THE **CONVERSATION!**

www.twitter.com/AlvinSlaughter—share and discover what's happening right now anywhere in the world.

ENJOY THE **RESTORATION!**

www.hopeforthemarriage.net—nationally recognized marriage resource. You can save your marriage, starting today, even if you are the only one interested, with this radical approach to marital rescue.

ENJOY THE **COMMUNICATION!**

www.ShareGodsLoveWithCards.net— changing lives…one card at a time!

ENJOY THE **FINANCIAL FREEDOM!**

www.zipdebtfree.com—debt elimination solutions. Learn the facts about your debt elimination solutions.

www.newlifedebtsolutions.com—at last, a simple step-by-step video to help YOU determine if debt settlement is the best strategy for you.